PREPARING FOR SUCCESS

A Guide for Teaching Adult English Language Learners

TABLE OF CONTENTS

ACKNOWLEDGEMENTS

Thanks are due to many people and programs for this book.

I'd like to thank Shirley Brod, Allene Grognet, and the Spring Institute for International Studies, Denver, Colorado, who contributed to and supported earlier versions of the book.

Deborah Kennedy, Key Resources, Inc., Washington, DC, made significant contributions to the form and content of the book.

Thanks are also due to Lisa Agao, CBET Curriculum Coordinator, Cesar Chavez Adult Education Center, Fresno, California; Jean Owensby, Coordinator, Los Angeles Adult and Career Education, California; Donna Moss, Project Coordinator, PBS, Literacy Link, Alexandria, Virginia; and Carol Van Duzer, Research Associate, Center for Applied Linguistics, Washington, DC, who reviewed earlier versions of this book and made significant contributions to the final product.

Lynn Fischer, Center for Applied Linguistics, Washington, DC, contributed significantly through administrative support and editorial assistance.

Finally, Miriam Burt, Center for Applied Linguistics, Washington, DC, shepherded the project from its inception to this finished product.

INTRODUCTION

Teachers of adults learning English in the United States are more than just language teachers. While they are preparing their students to be successful on the job and in the community, they must meet the needs of a variety of stakeholders: the learners, the employers, the community, and the funding agencies. This book describes the policy initiatives and economic realities that are influencing program design and demonstrates how the agendas of each of the stakeholders can be reconciled in a way that renders them mutually supportive. Rather than focusing on the differences in expected outcomes, the book focuses on the commonalties among the goals of the stakeholders. It equips the instructor to provide quality learner-centered instruction while responding to the full range of current programmatic demands, including assessing and responding to student-identified learning objectives, providing students with the skills that employers are demanding, and documenting student outcomes through standardized assessment procedures.

Section 1 sets the scene by describing the forces that are shaping program design and administration. Section 2 provides practical suggestions on how to assess the needs of the various stakeholders. Section 3 gives strategies for reconciling the agendas of the stakeholders. Section 4 presents ways to convey workplace and civics competencies through the instructional process. Section 5 discusses how to convey behavioral expectations through classroom management techniques. Section 6 offers suggestions for helping learners develop lifelong learning skills.

As instructors incorporate the practical activities described in these pages, they will be preparing their learners for success by enabling them to respond appropriately and effectively to the expectations of the community, the educational system, and the workplace. This book includes many forms and activities for use in the classroom. Teachers can adapt them to meet the needs of their students and to fit the classroom contexts.

SECTION ONE

Factors Influencing Program Design

Legislative Requirements and Labor Market Realities

What has generated the pressure on program staff to meet both learners' language needs and employers' and communities' requirements? The answer lies in a number of factors, including the labor market, workplace demands, welfare-to-work initiatives, and the emphasis in adult education and training programs on performance-based accountability.

The Labor Market

A recent Educational Testing Service (ETS) report, *Getting Down to Business: Matching Welfare Recipients' Skills to Jobs That Train* (Carnevale & Desrochers, 1999), found that although the flourishing economy of the 1990s created enough jobs to absorb individuals with higher skills, the prospects for those with low skills are bleak and will only become bleaker. As Barton and Jenkins (1995) note, "Levels of literacy and degree of success in the labor market are clearly and closely linked" (p. 8). Fewer and fewer jobs are available to persons with low language skills, and the jobs that are available do not pay a living wage. In such a context, individuals who demonstrate language and literacy skills below the level of the least skilled workers "may get work, but their earnings will not keep them out of poverty and their employment future remains precarious" (D'Amico, 1997, p. 5).

Workplace Demands and SCANS

In March 2001, the American Management Association (AMA) published findings from a survey of over 1,000 personnel executives (http://www.amanet.org/research/pdfs/bjp_2001.pdf). The report stated that more than a third of job applicants nationwide lacked the requisite math and reading skills to do the jobs they were seeking, up from 19% in 1996. The sharp increase was attributed to the higher skill levels required in today's workplace, where new technologies have raised the bar for job applicants in terms of literacy and math.

The AMA survey confirmed a trend that was observed and documented by the Secretary's Commission on Achieving Necessary Skills (SCANS), a group of prominent educators and representatives from business and labor convened by the U.S. Department of Labor in 1990. The Commission was asked to determine what work requires of schools. After talking with business owners, public employers, managers, union officials, and desk and line workers in stores, government offices, and manufacturing facilities, the SCANS (1991) concluded the following:

> Good jobs depend on people who can put knowledge to work. New workers must be creative and responsible problem solvers and have the skills and attitudes on which employers can build. Traditional jobs are changing and new jobs are created every day. High paying but unskilled jobs are disappearing. Employers and employees share the belief that all workplaces must work smarter. (p. v)

In *What Work Requires of Schools* (1991), the Commission identified a set of five competencies, which, based on a three-part foundation of skills, lie at the heart of effective job performance (see Figures 1.1 and 1.2).

Figure 1.1
SCANS Three-Part Foundation of Skills and Personal Qualities

Basic Skills: Reads, writes, performs arithmetic and mathematical operations, listens and speaks

Reading – locates, understands, and interprets written information in prose and in documents such as manuals, graphs, and schedules

Writing – communicates thoughts, ideas, information, and messages in writing; creates documents such as letters, directions, manuals, reports, graphs, and flow charts.

Arithmetic/Mathematics – performs basic computations and approaches practical problems by choosing appropriately from a variety of mathematical techniques

Listening – receives, attends to, interprets, and responds to verbal messages and other cues

Speaking – organizes ideas and communicates orally

Thinking Skills: Thinks creatively, makes decisions, solves problems, visualizes, knows how to learn, and reasons

Creative Thinking – generates new ideas

Decision Making – specifies goals and constraints, generates alternatives, considers risks, and evaluates and chooses best alternative

Problem Solving – recognizes problems and devises and implements plan of action

Seeing Things in the Mind's Eye – organizes and processes symbols, pictures, graphs, objects, and other information

Knowing How to Learn – uses efficient learning techniques to acquire and apply new knowledge and skills

Reasoning – discovers a rule or principle underlying the relationship between two or more objects and applies it when solving a problem

Personal Qualities: Displays responsibility, self-esteem, sociability, self-management, and integrity and honesty

Responsibility – exerts a high level of effort and perseveres towards goal attainment

Self-Esteem – believes in own self-worth and maintains a positive view of self

Sociability – demonstrates understanding, friendliness, adaptability, empathy, and politeness in group settings

Self-Management – assesses self accurately, sets personal goals, monitors progress, and exhibits self-control

Integrity/Honesty – chooses ethical courses of action

From *What Work Requires of Schools*, by Secretary's Commission on Achieving Necessary Skills, 1991, Washington, DC: U.S. Department of Labor. Available: http://wdr.doleta.gov/SCANS/whatwork/whatwork.html

Figure 1.2
Five SCANS Competencies

Resources: Identifies, organizes, plans, and allocates resources

Time – Selects goal-relevant activities, ranks them, allocates time, and prepares and follows schedules

Money – Uses or prepares budgets, makes forecasts, keeps records, and makes adjustments to meet objectives

Materials and Facilities – Acquires, stores, allocates, and uses materials or space efficiently

Human Resources – Assesses skills and distributes work accordingly, evaluates performance and provides feedback

Interpersonal: Works with others

Participates as Member of a Team – contributes to group effort

Teaches Others New Skills

Serves Clients/Customers – works to satisfy customer's expectations

Exercises Leadership – communicates ideas to justify position, persuades and convinces others, responsibly challenges existing procedures and policies

Negotiates – works toward agreements involving exchange of resources, resolves divergent interests

Works with Diversity – works well with men and women from diverse backgrounds

Information: Acquires and uses information

Acquires and Evaluates Information

Organizes and Maintains Information

Interprets and Communicates Information

Uses Computers to Process Information

Systems: Understands complex inter-relationships

Understands Systems – knows how social, organizational, and technological systems work and operates effectively with them

Monitors and Corrects Performance – distinguishes trends, predicts impacts on system operations, diagnoses deviations in systems' performance and corrects malfunctions

Improves or Designs Systems – suggests modifications to existing systems and develops new or alternative systems to improve performance

Technology: Works with a variety of technologies

Selects Technology – chooses procedures, tools, or equipment including computers and related technologies

Applies Technology to Task – Understands overall intent and proper procedures for setup and operation of equipment

Maintains and Troubleshoots Equipment – Prevents, identifies, and solves problems with equipment, including computers and other technologies

From *What Work Requires of Schools*, by Secretary's Commission on Achieving Necessary Skills, 1991, Washington, DC: U.S. Department of Labor. Available: http://wdr.doleta.gov/SCANS/whatwork/whatwork.html

Subsequent SCANS publications, including *Teaching the SCANS Competencies* (SCANS, 1993), were designed to guide educators in the creation of classroom-based opportunities to develop the SCANS competencies and foundation skills. The Commission stated that the competencies and foundation skills should be taught and understood in an integrated fashion that reflected the nature of the workplace contexts in which they would be applied, stressing the following three principles:

1. **The primary place to teach SCANS is within existing curricula.**

> The skills identified by SCANS as necessary for work are already taught to a limited extent in existing courses. . . . But even when such knowledge is embedded in the current curriculum, it typically is not made intellectually explicit. . . . When such connections are not made explicit, students are less likely to generalize skills and knowledge and to apply them in new situations.
>
> It is especially important to connect knowledge and skills to the workplace so that students can see how they will use them. (SCANS, 1993, p. 15)

2. **Students should be active participants in their own learning.**

> In the view of the Commission, students do not learn to grapple with problems and to apply skills if teachers are always directing the learning and doing the talking. Working together on problems, students are more responsible for their own learning, more actively involved. Most importantly, they are functioning as they will in the workplace. (p. 15)

3. **Instructors should design instructional tasks and problems that require learners to employ a range of skills.**

> In the workplace, we do not use one skill at a time in isolation from other skills; effective performance requires many different skills used in combination. It stands to reason, then, that students benefit from working on tasks and problems that call on a range of skills. (p. 15)

Thus, the findings and recommendations of the SCANS may influence what employers and funding agencies expect adult education programs to implement.

Welfare-to-Work Initiatives

Federal welfare reform legislation, the Personal Responsibility and Work Opportunities Reconciliation Act (PRWORA), was enacted in 1996 (http://www.acf.dhhs.gov/programs/cse/fct/irspam.htm). This legislation ended an entitlement approach to public assistance and created a new focus on workforce participation. An application for assistance from the welfare program now prompts the delivery of a range of services designed to promote swift entry or reentry into the workforce. The stated aim of the legislation is to encourage personal responsibility and self-sufficiency.

However, an Educational Testing System (ETS) report (Carnevale & Desrochers, 1999) documents a stark mismatch between many welfare recipients' skills and the skills required for jobs that lead to self-sufficiency. The report finds that, while the lowest paid jobs provide work experience, they typically offer little further training. Consequently, more time on the job does not appreciably increase low-skilled workers' opportunities for advancement and increased earnings.

The problem documented in the report is corroborated in *Workforce Literacy* (n.d.), a fact sheet compiled by the National Institute for Literacy (NIFL) (http://www.nifl.gov/newworld/WORKFORC.HTM). Of more than 300 executives surveyed, 71% reported that basic written communication training was critical to meeting their workplaces' changing skill demands. However, only 26% of the companies offered this kind of training. In addition, 47% of the executives reported the need for workers to improve basic math skills, but only 5% of the companies offered basic math skills training. With so little opportunity for skills training at the worksite, learners turn to adult education programs to provide what they need.

Performance-Based Accountability and NRS

In 1995, the U.S. Congress was considering eliminating adult education as a separate delivery system and integrating it into a general system of workforce development. To provide a rationale for retaining and funding adult education as a separate program, legislators demanded convincing data on the impact of adult education at the state and federal levels. In response to these demands, the U.S. Department of Education's Division of Adult Education and Literacy expanded the development of its indicators of program quality initiative into a national system for collecting uniform and consistent information on adult education learner outcomes. The result, the National Reporting System for Adult Education (NRS), was formally instituted in 1997 (http://www.air-dc.org/nrs/).

In August 1998, the Adult Education and Family Literacy Act (AEFLA), Title II of the Workforce Investment Act of 1998, became law. The AEFLA established accountability requirements for states receiving federal funds for adult education. The NRS became the vehicle for states to report their outcome-based performance data. It identifies five core outcome measures that address the AEFLA requirements for core performance indicators:

1. Educational gain (skills to advance educational functioning level)
2. Employment
3. Employment retention
4. Placement in postsecondary education or training
5. Receipt of a secondary school diploma or GED

For the first of these outcome measures, *educational gain*, NRS identifies six functioning levels for English-as-a-second-language (ESL) students. Each level describes the skills and competencies that a learner at that level possesses across three skill areas: speaking and listening, basic reading and writing, and functional and workplace skills. Using the NRS descriptors as guidelines, local programs assess learners at intake to determine their baseline educational level. The program may select the skill areas in which to assess learners based on the learners' instructional needs and goals. After a predetermined amount of instruction or time, the program assesses learners in the same skill areas and uses the educational functioning level descriptors to determine whether each learner has advanced one or more levels. The National Reporting System for Adult Education (2001) specifies that "state and local programs may use any assessment procedures desired, as long as the procedures are standardized for all programs in the same way" (p. 19). This means that states could choose to require all programs within that state to use a standardized test, such as the Basic English Skills Test (BEST, http://www.cal.org/BEST/) or the CASAS Life Skills tests (http://www.casas.org/). This is the option that states such as California and Texas have chosen. States also have the option to use performance assessments as their assessment procedure, providing the procedure is standardized for all programs in the same way and has standardized scoring protocols. For example, Ohio initially assesses learners with a standardized test to determine entry level and is developing a uniform portfolio system of performance assessments to assess level gain. States may use additional educational levels and skill area descriptors, as long as they are compatible with NRS levels and skills (see Figure 1.3).

Figure 1.3
Three NRS Educational Functional Levels

	Beginning ESL Literacy	Low Intermediate ESL	High Advanced ESL
Speaking and Listening	• Individual cannot speak or understand English or understands only isolated words or phrases.	• Individual can understand simple learned phrases and limited new phrases containing familiar vocabulary spoken slowly with frequent repetition. • Individual can ask and respond to questions using such phrases. • Individual can express basic survival needs and participate in some routine social conversations, although with some difficulty. • Individual has some control of basic grammar.	• Individual can understand and participate effectively in face-to-face conversations on everyday subjects spoken at normal speed. • Individual can converse and understand independently in survival, work, and social situations. • Individual can expand on basic ideas in conversation, but with some hesitation. • Individual can clarify general meaning and control basic grammar, although still lacks total control over complex structures.
Basic Reading and Writing	• Individual has no or minimal reading or writing skills in any language. • Individual may have little or no comprehension of how print corresponds to spoken language and may have difficulty using a writing instrument.	• Individual can read simple material on familiar subjects and comprehend simple and compound sentences in single or linked paragraphs containing familiar vocabulary. • Individual can write simple notes and messages on familiar situations, but lacks clarity and focus. • Sentence structure lacks variety but shows some control of basic grammar (e.g., present and past tense) and consistent use of punctuation (e.g., periods, capitalization).	• Individual can read authentic materials on everyday subjects and can handle most reading related to life roles. • Individual can consistently and fully interpret descriptive narratives on familiar topics and gain meaning from unfamiliar topics. • Individual uses increased control of language and meaning-making strategies to gain meaning of unfamiliar texts. • Individual can write multiparagraph essays with a clear introduction and development of ideas. • Writing contains well formed sentences, appropriate mechanics and spelling, and few grammatical errors.
Functional and Workplace Skills	• Individual functions minimally or not at all in English and can communicate only through gestures or a few isolated words, such as name and other personal information. • Individual may recognize only common signs or symbols (e.g., stop sign, product logos). • Individual can handle only very routine entry-level jobs that do not require oral or written communication in English. • There is no knowledge or use of computers or technology.	• Individual can interpret simple directions and schedules, signs and maps. • Individual can fill out simple forms, but needs support on some documents that are not simplified. • Individual can handle routine entry level jobs that involve some written or oral English communication, but in which job tasks can be demonstrated. • Individual can use simple computer programs and can perform a sequence of routine tasks given directions using technology (e.g., fax machine, computer).	• Individual has a general ability to use English effectively to meet most routine social and work situations. • Individual can interpret routine charts, graphs, and tables and complete forms. • Individual has high ability to communicate on the telephone and understand radio and television. • Individual can meet work demands that require reading and writing and can interact with the public. • Individual can use common software and learn new applications. • Individual can define purpose of software and select new applications appropriately. • Individual can instruct others in use of software and technology.

The above information and information about the remaining three levels can be accessed on the NRS Web site at http://www.oei-tech.com/NRS/

The remaining four core outcome measures apply to learners who enter a program with goals related to those specific measures. For learners who enter a program with the goal of obtaining employment, there are two measures: *employment* (the student obtains a job in the first quarter after leaving the instructional program) and *retained employment* (the student still has a job in the third quarter after exiting the instructional program). The latter measure also applies to learners who are employed when they enter a program.

The last two measures apply to learners whose goals include *advancing to further education* or *obtaining a secondary school diploma or GED*. To report on each of these measures, program staff record learners' goals upon entry and track achievement of each stated goal.

Definitions of Success

The legislative requirements and labor market realities have had a profound impact on ESL service providers' understanding of what success is, both for their learners and for their programs. In addition, adult ESL programs find that learners, the central stakeholders, have their own definitions of success and their own sets of demands and expectations for instructional programs. These may be predicated on the requirements for full participation in civic and community life as well as in the workforce, reflecting what a report by the National Research Council called "the complexities of contemporary life" (Bransford, Brown, & Cockings, 1999). The report continues,

> The skill demands for work have increased dramatically, as has the need for organizations and workers to change in response to competitive workplace pressures. Thoughtful participation in the democratic process has also become increasingly complicated as the focus of attention has shifted from local to national and global concerns. Above all, information and knowledge are growing at a far more rapid rate than ever before in the history of humankind . . . the meaning of "knowing" has shifted from being able to remember and repeat information to being able to find and use it. (pp. 3-4)

In designing instruction for adult ESL learners then, providers must navigate between different sets of expectations to produce outcomes that are recognized as successful by all the critical stakeholders.

What Employers Say

As learners' current and future employers, businesses have a stake in learners' success. They are concerned about workers having the language, literacy, and math skills at certain levels to do the job required.

What Policy Says

As the source of funding support for both learners on welfare and the programs that serve them, the federal government also has a stake in learners' success, which it defines in terms of states' implementation of the National Reporting System.

What Learners Say

In 1994, the National Institute for Literacy (NIFL) launched the Equipped for the Future (EFF) initiative in response to the National Education Goals Panel challenge for a literate nation by the year 2000 (National Education Goals Panel, 1993). NIFL sent an open letter to teachers, tutors, and adult learners across the country, inviting them to answer the question behind Goal 6: What is it that adults need to know and be able to do in order to be literate, compete in the global economy, exercise the rights and responsibilities of citizenship and participate fully in their children's education? This research effort aimed to map the critical responsibilities of family, civic, and work life from the perspective of adult learners. EFF categorized the needs reported by adult learners into the following four fundamental areas:

EFF Four Purposes for Learning

(http://www.nifl.gov/lincs/collections/eff/purposes.html)

1. **ACCESS** to information and resources so adults can orient themselves in the world.
2. **VOICE** to express ideas and opinions with the confidence that one will be heard and taken into account.
3. **ACTION** to be able to solve problems and make decisions, acting independently.
4. **BRIDGE TO THE FUTURE** to learn how to learn in order to keep up with the world as it changes.

Figure 1.4
EFF Content Standards

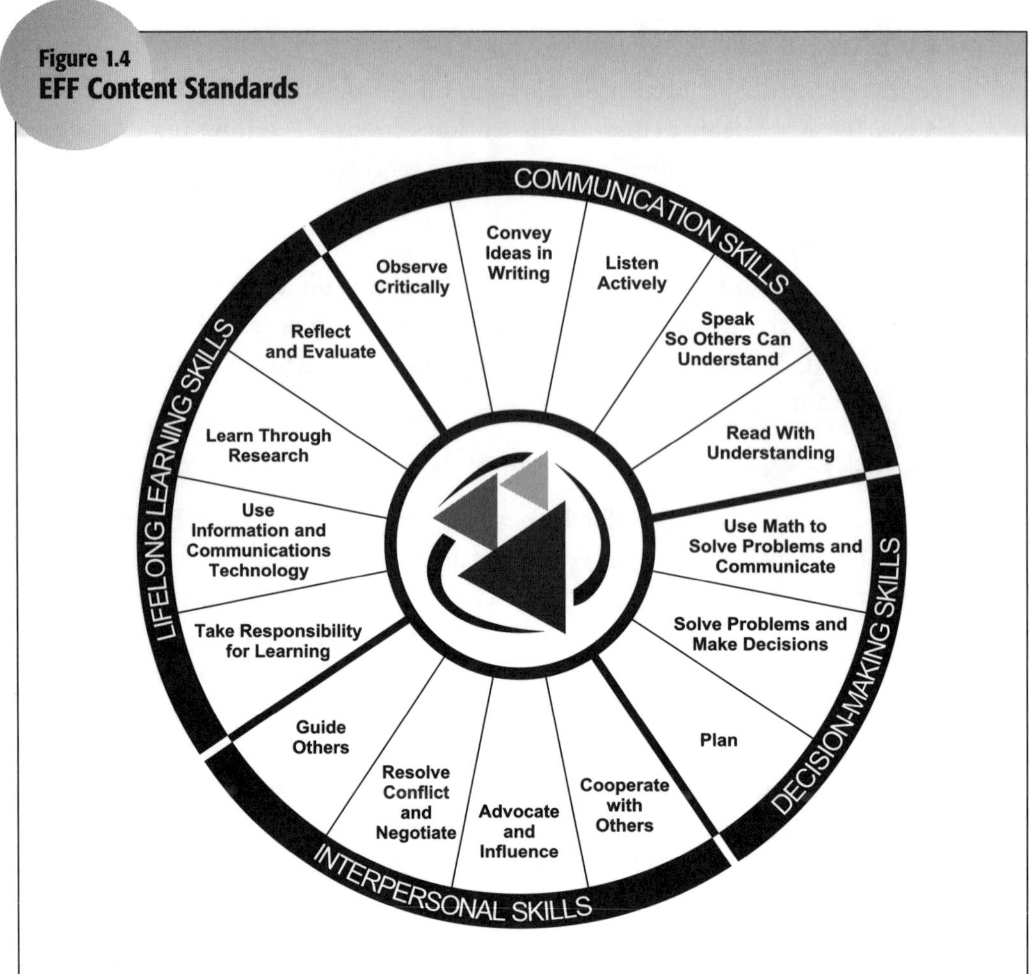

http://www.nifl.gov/lincs/collections/eff/eff_standards.html

NIFL presents these Four Purposes as the basis of a "customer-driven mandate for change" (Stein, 2000, p. 2) to guide the adult education field in its efforts to equip students with the skills they need to achieve Goal 6. A core set of 16 skill standards, which constitute a foundation for success in managing today's world and in preparing for the future, were identified (Figure 1.4). EFF hopes these standards will (a) encourage adult learners and their teachers to think about strategies for learning the necessary skills, (b) fulfill the learners' purposes, and (c) identify barriers to learning and establish strategies for getting past them.

EFF presents a framework that adults can use to assess their own knowledge and skills in relation to their personal and career goals so they can shape a course that will better prepare them for the future. Teachers and instructional programs can also use this framework to link curriculum and instruction, as well as assessment and evaluation, to achievement of real-world outcomes.

EFF and SCANS

Interestingly, although the SCANS and the EFF initiatives were started at different times and developed from different perspectives, they yielded conclusions that are remarkably similar and mutually supportive. SCANS asked from the perspective of employers, "What does work require of schools?" EFF asked from the perspective of adult learners, "What is it that adults need to know and be able to do in the 21st century?" Although the competencies and foundation skills identified and documented by SCANS were presented as the bedrock of effective job performance, their relevance to and support of other domains of adult learners' lives is evident and is in harmony with the rationale for the design of the 16 EFF Standards. For example,

> EFF Standards encourage a problem-solving approach to skill development. While the focus of teaching and assessment is on what students need to learn in a particular situation to achieve their purpose, the goal is longer term: to build, over time, the cognitive and metacognitive strategies that facilitate learning with understanding and transfer of learning from one context to another. (Stein, 2000, p. 20)

This statement resonates with many of the skills and competencies highlighted by SCANS, such as

- **Thinking Skills.** Thinks creatively, makes decisions, solves problems, visualizes, knows how to learn and reason.
- **Decision Making.** Specifies goals and constraints, generates alternatives, considers risks, and evaluates and chooses the best alternative.
- **Problem Solving.** Recognizes problems and devises and implements a plan of action.
- **Knowing How to Learn.** Uses efficient learning techniques to acquire and apply new knowledge and skills.
- **Self-Management.** Assesses self accurately, sets personal goals, monitors progress, and exhibits self-control.

- **Leadership Skills.** Communicates ideas to justify position, persuades and convinces others, responsibly challenges existing procedures and policies.
- **Negotiation.** Works toward agreements involving exchanges or resources; resolves divergent interests.

What Programs Can Do

Now that the agendas of legislative requirements, labor market realities, and the learners have been acknowledged, program staff must determine how to design their program to meet the needs and wants of their particular stakeholders. Section 2 provides practical suggestions for assessing stakeholder needs.

SECTION TWO

Assessing Needs

A variety of expectations, frameworks, guidelines, and requirements often govern the assessment of learners' needs and the shape of the instruction designed to meet these needs. Thomas Hutchinson (as cited in Vella, 1994) describes this complex situation in terms of Who needs What as defined by Whom? In his model, the "Who" are the learners, the "What" are learners' needs, and the "Whom" are those who define the "What." When curriculum content, materials, and teaching approaches are responsive to learners' self-perceived needs, learners are more likely to be motivated and ultimately successful. However, as pointed out in the previous section, learners' needs may also be dictated by adult-education-agency standards, employment possibilities, employer expectations, community-participation obligations, and the priorities and standards of funding agencies.

Assessment of Learners' Needs and Expectations

Adult educator Malcolm Knowles stressed the importance of providing instruction that addresses the needs and interests of adult learners. In his introduction to *Andragogy in Action* (1984), he presents an instructional model that builds on the following assumptions:

- Adults are self-directed learners.
- Adults have a rich reservoir of experience that can serve as a resource for learning.
- Since adults' readiness to learn is frequently affected by their need to know or do something, they tend to have a life-centered, task-centered, or problem-centered orientation to learning as opposed to a subject-matter orientation.
- Adults are generally motivated to learn due to internal or intrinsic factors (such as being able to help their children with homework) as opposed to external or extrinsic forces (such as a raise in salary).

Adult ESL learners often fit this model. They come to an ESL program with a self-identified agenda or motivation. They know why they are studying English. It may be because they want to communicate with their American-born grandchildren, or travel around the city on their own, or understand what their co-workers are talking about on breaks, or obtain work in a specific field.

However, not all adult learners' agendas or motivations are so clearly defined; some learners are unable to get beyond, "I want to learn more English." When learners lack the basic functional skills or knowledge necessary to articulate specific goals, the effectiveness of learner-centered instruction is reduced because learners are not self-directed. Instructors need to provide intensive support that will help learners first recognize and describe their needs so that they can then develop specific goals.

At other times, the agenda and motivation of learners can be at odds with those of the funding agency that referred them to the ESL class. For example, welfare recipients may be referred to an ESL class by a welfare agency whose primary goal is for those individuals to acquire work-related oral language skills as quickly as possible to secure employment. The learners, on the other hand, may want to develop comprehensive language and literacy skills that would make higher level education and training and better paying jobs more accessible. These mismatched goals can have an impact on an individual's motivation to succeed.

Needs assessments can help determine the degree of direction and support that will benefit learners most. Weddel and Van Duzer (1997) describe *needs assessment* for adult ESL learners as,

> a tool that examines, from the perspective of the learner, what kinds of English, native language, and literacy skills the learner already believes he or she has; the literacy contexts in which the learner lives and works; what the learner wants and needs to know to function in those contexts; what the learner expects to gain from the instructional program; and what might need to be done in the native language or with the aid of an interpreter. (p. 1)

They identify the following purposes for needs assessment:

- providing information to instructors and learners about what learners bring to the classroom, what has been accomplished previously, and what learners want and need to know;
- increasing the likelihood of an emergent curriculum that is responsive to learner needs and wants rather than a predetermined and fixed curriculum informed only by instructors' perspectives; and
- aiding in the development of appropriate and effective materials, resources, skills assessments, teaching approaches, and teacher training.

Needs assessment should not be limited to the beginning of an instructional session or the first week of an individual's participation in a particular class. Instructors can use ongoing needs assessment as an integral part of their instructional approach to allow for new and emerging issues:

> At the beginning of the program, needs assessment might be used to determine appropriate program types and course content; during the program, it assures that learner and program goals are being met and allows for necessary program changes; at the end of the program, it can be used for assessing progress and planning future directions for the learners and the program. (Weddel & Van Duzer, 1997, p. 1)

Individual needs assessments that are accessible to learners at all levels of English language and literacy can easily be developed and integrated into regular classroom instruction. Some of the more typical needs assessment instruments and activities include the following:

- **Survey questionnaires.** Surveys can include a list of topics, skills, or language and literacy uses. Learners can be asked to rank them; select areas that are of importance, interest, or need; and identify areas that are of less importance or have already been mastered.
- **Picture-interest inventories.** Picture inventories are especially useful for beginning learners and for those with minimal literacy in their own language. A series of pictures, showing activities and contexts in which English language and literacy may be needed, form the basis for determining the areas of greatest interest and the motivation behind a student's presence in class. Learners are asked to organize and categorize the picture series in different ways, such as "things you need to do every day and things you need to do only sometimes" or "things that you find easy to do and things that are harder to do."
- **Picture prompts.** In this activity, a few pictures of adults in different situations are used to generate class discussion. Students are asked to identify what the individuals in the pictures are doing and what they might talk about or write about in each situation. Students are then asked if they need or want to be able to do these things themselves.
- **Learner interviews.** Conducting informal one-on-one or small-group interviews with students, either in English or in their native language, is an excellent strategy for determining what students already know, their primary reason for enrollment, and the ways in which they need or want to use English language and literacy.

- **Reading material review.** Instructors can use a wide variety of reading material as the basis for needs determination, including the telephone directory, a VCR manual, a newspaper, a letter from a child's school, a label from a toxic household substance, a telephone bill, a parking citation, and a bus schedule. Instructors can ask learners to identify the reading matter that is of most interest, most difficult, or most important for them.
- **Language logs or journals.** Periodically, students can be asked to write about recent situations in which they needed to use oral English language or writing skills. For higher level students this might be a regular focused journal-writing activity in which students respond to a prompt such as, "The most important reason I needed to use English this week was...." Lower level students might be asked to complete the sentence, "Yesterday I needed to speak English when...."
- **Language-use inventories.** Learners can be asked to keep lists of the ways they use language and literacy, and classroom time can be assigned on a regular basis for updating the lists.
- **Work-related interest inventories.** The language-learning environment can be a useful forum for the discovery of work-related interests and aptitudes. Work-related interest inventories that involve learners in identifying the qualities of different kinds of employment can help to determine and prioritize the specific areas of language and literacy on which they should focus. For example, a simple "like" and "dislike" choice made about pictures that show a range of jobs can be used as the basis for determining what employment features are appealing. Is it outdoor work with tools or work that involves interaction with others that is represented in the "like" pile?

Worksheets 2.1 through 2.8 are examples of worksheets that can be used with these activities.

WORKSHEET 2.1

Work-Related Interest Inventory

For each job, check like  ***or don't like*** 

Then talk to a classmate. Explain why you checked like or don't like.

carpenter ______ ______

hairdresser ______ ______

computer technician ______ ______

painter ______ ______

teacher ______ ______

doctor ______ ______

waitress/waiter ______ ______

construction worker ______ ______

mechanic ______ ______

bus driver ______ ______

WORKSHEET 2.2

Survey Questionnaire: Beginning Level

In English class I want to

WRITE	READ
SPEAK How are you? Fine, thank you	LISTEN
 HOUSE PRACTICE PRONUNCIATION	① First __________ ② Second __________ ③ Third __________ ④ Fourth __________ ⑤ Fifth __________

Donna Moss: TESOL 94: Alternative Assessment: A Fork in the Road (used with permission)

WORKSHEET 2.3

Picture-Interest Inventory

Name ____________________ Circle (5) you need to study.

Classroom and housing	Holidays
ABC It's on the sofa Where is the book?	I LOVE YOU

Time and weather	Money
What time is it? It's 2:00 It's windy and raining.	dollar bill - 25¢ Do you have change for a dollar? yes, I do

Community	Consumerism
LIBRARY BANK The library is next to the bank I need 3 29¢ stamps	50.00 apple hat grapes jacket I need a pound of onions They are 59¢ a pound

Health	Transportation
arm leg I have a stomachache. 911	I walk to school Bus Stop

Donna Moss: TESOL 94: Alternative Assessment: A Fork in the Road (used with permission)

WORKSHEET 2.4

Survey Questionnaire: Intermediate/Advanced Level

Name____ Date______________

1. Please explain why you need more English. Be specific with examples of situations which are difficult for you now.

2. What problem area do you want to improve before you leave this class?

3. When people speak English to you, do you understand:
_____ 100% _____ 80% _____ 65% _____ 50% _____ less than 50%

4. When you speak English, do people understand you:
_____ 100% _____ 80% _____ 65% _____ 50% _____ less than 50%

5. When you watch TV, how much do you understand?
_____ everything _____ most _____ some _____ a little _____ very little

6. Please **ORDER** the skills that you need from 1 to 6. **Number 1** is the **most important** and **6** is the **least important** to you at this time. **Please use each number only once.**

_____ READING
_____ WRITING
_____ LISTENING
_____ SPEAKING
_____ VOCABULARY
_____ PRONUNCIATION

7. Have you ever studied English in the past? ___ yes ___ no How long? ________

Where? ___________________________ When? ___________________________

Donna Moss: TESOL 94: Alternative Assessment: A Fork in the Road (used with permission)

WORKSHEET 2.5

Learner Interview

Reading

Group Members: ______________________________

____

In your groups, **discuss the following questions**:

1. What kinds of things do you read in English at home or at work?

2. How do you read? Do you read for a short time or a long time? Do you stop in the middle to think about your reading? What environment do you like when you are reading?

1. ______________________________
2. ______________________________
3. ______________________________
4. ______________________________
5. ______________________________

3. What kinds of things do you like to read?

4. What kind of things do you expect to read when you go on to college or vocational training? How do you think it might be different from now?

5. What kinds of problems do you experience when you read? Why is each one a problem? Discuss any or all of the following:

- Vocabulary
- Using a dictionary quickly and efficiently
- Sentence structure
- Technical language
- Unknown subjects
- Remembering previous reading
- Putting the overall meaning together
- Understanding the writer's purpose
- Understanding the main idea
- Distinguishing between fact or fiction
- Other: ______________________________

____

5. Discuss some possible solutions for these problems:

PROBLEM ______________ **SOLUTION** ______________

______________ ______________

Sharon McKay: TESOL 94: Alternative Assessment: A Fork in the Road (used with permission)

WORKSHEET 2.6

Language Log

Name____ Date______________

Where did you speak English this week?

____

____

____

Who did you speak English to?

____

____

____

What did you read in English this week?

____

____

____

This week I needed to study ____

____

____

This week ____ was difficult in class.

This week ____ was easy in class.

You are doing great work in English!

Donna Moss: TESOL 94: Alternative Assessment: A Fork in the Road (used with permission)

WORKSHEET 2.7

Language-Use Inventory

Answer for YOU

	Who did you speak to?	**What did you say?**	**Was it easy? Was it difficult?**
At home?			Easy A little difficult Difficult
At work?			Easy A little difficult Difficult
At the store?			Easy A little difficult Difficult

Ask your PARTNER

	Who did you speak to?	**What did you say?**	**Was it easy? Was it difficult?**
At home?			Easy A little difficult Difficult
At work?			Easy A little difficult Difficult
At the store?			Easy A little difficult Difficult

Donna Moss: TESOL 94: Alternative Assessment: A Fork in the Road (used with permission)

WORKSHEET 2.8

Survey Questionnaire: Ranking

Read the following topics. Order the topics that you would like to study.
1 is the **MOST IMPORTANT** and **10** is the **LEAST IMPORTANT**.

____ STUDY AND LEARNING STRATEGIES: How do you study reading material, your notes, graphs, tables, etc? How do you preview, skim, and scan reading material?

____ TEST-TAKING SKILLS: How do you prepare, study for, and take standardized tests?

____ THE WRITING PROCESS: How do you brainstorm, organize, develop topic sentences, write, revise, and edit your writing?

____ NOTE-TAKING SKILLS: How do you take effective notes from lectures and written material?

____ CAREER PLANNING: How do you investigate and decide on a career path or plan for the future?

____ BUILDING VOCABULARY: How do you understand new vocabulary when you are reading? How do you study vocabulary so that you can remember it?

____ USING REFERENCE MATERIALS: How do you effectively use the dictionary, thesaurus, newspapers, magazines, and other reference materials?

____ USING THE LIBRARY: How do you best use the local, school, or technical library to research for needed information?

_____ SPEAKING: GIVING ORAL PRESENTATION or MAKING PHONE CONTACTS: How do you research, organize, and give oral presentations? How do you improve listening comprehension and speaking fluency in telephone conversations?

Donna Moss: TESOL 94: Alternative Assessment: A Fork in the Road (used with permission)

Assessment of the Employment Context

Although ESL students may not specify employment-related reasons as their primary motivation for attending ESL classes, both those who are currently employed and those who intend to seek employment may identify general language and literacy skills that are, in fact, related directly or indirectly to their employment goals. For example, when questioned for details as to why they want to improve their speaking skills, learners often indicate a desire to communicate better with individuals such as supervisors or co-workers. The goal of attaining a high school diploma or general equivalency degree (GED) is also generally related to improved employment prospects. These employment-related skills can be easily integrated into instructional content and practice.

In order to integrate an appropriate employment focus into instruction, ESL instructors need to understand the needs and expectations of the local job market. A number of sources are available to help instructors. The competencies outlined in the EFF and SCANS documents provide a general picture of employers' requirements and expectations for their workers. To gain in-depth knowledge of specific companies or work environments, instructors can use the following strategies:

Employer phone interviews based on EFF and SCANS competencies.

Many human resources personnel may never have heard of SCANS or EFF, but they are usually pleased to talk with instructors when they understand that the focus of the conversation is how to include workplace competencies in ESL instruction. Instructors may be surprised by the answers to questions such as, "What kind of things are you looking for in an effective employee?" "What kind of skills should I be emphasizing in the ESL classroom?" (The language that employers typically use often resembles that which appears in the EFF and SCANS publications.) These are some other questions that can yield useful information:

- What kind of reading and writing skills do your new hires need to demonstrate?
- How well do your employees need to speak English and understand spoken English?
- Do you encourage employees to pursue education and training opportunities?
- What are the most common reasons for letting people go?

- What qualities do you see in your best employees?
- Are there any safety issues connected to speaking and reading English in your workplace?
- How well do your employees need to speak, read, and write English for promotion opportunities?

Employer advisory committees. An employer advisory committee can provide a direct source of information on workplace trends. Employers can be invited to attend regular roundtable discussions with teachers and administrators. Some programs have found that, given the busy schedules of most employers, these may be successfully conducted as early-morning breakfast meetings.

Job shadowing. By spending a period of time in a workplace, instructors can observe interactions, organizational behavior, workplace procedures, and personnel issues. Job shadowing also provides the opportunity to observe language and literacy interactions in the workplace. (See Grognet, 1996, for more information on needs assessment at the workplace.)

Labor market surveys. As a condition for funding, many vocational training programs are required to keep labor market surveys on file. These are an excellent source of information on local economic trends, changes in the job market, and demand levels for various occupations.

Identifying Community Participation Issues

ESL teachers need to be aware of issues that affect a learner's ability to participate productively and equitably in the community. Teachers often act as so-called culture brokers for learners who use the ESL classroom as a source for cultural interpretation (Adkins & Berman, 1999). Although learners may not identify these issues during the course of needs assessment activities, instructors should be aware of the information needs and behavioral expectations that will be critical to a learner's successful participation in the wider community.

For example, a federal program that has potential benefits for learners working in entry-level or other low-paying positions is the Earned Income Tax Credit (EITC). The EITC can make the difference between a family eking out a subsistence existence and effectively making the transition from welfare reliance or low-income wages to a higher standard of living (Council of Economic Advisors, 1998). Yet learners may have never heard of the EITC, since employers are under no obligation to inform workers of their right to claim it. In addition, needs assessments may not have generated any requests for information on making low-income work livable. The instructor should determine to what extent this issue is relevant and whether to include it in the instructional program. The School of Continuing Education at Santa Ana College (California) developed instructional materials to familiarize English language learners with the EITC. (For information on how to order these materials, see Additional Resources.)

Additionally, ESL instructors need to be aware of the diverse issues that learners are likely to encounter in the workplace. For example, an ESL class that is serving highly educated refugees and immigrants will need a different focus from one that is serving agricultural workers with limited education in their country of origin. Both groups might benefit from EITC information, but the learners with professional qualifications from their countries of origin might also benefit from ESL instruction that includes information on licensing procedures in the United States and getting credentials verified and accepted. The learners from agricultural backgrounds, on the other hand, might benefit from ESL instruction that includes information on high school diploma and GED programs and vocational training opportunities. From 1996 to 1998, the International Institute of St. Louis operated Special Targeted Assistance for Refugees (STAR), a project funded by the Office of Refugee Resettlement. The goals of the project included recredentialing refugee professionals and counseling individuals about appropriate educational resources.

Listed below are other community and life-skills topics that may be of benefit to adult learners.

- Low-cost health insurance for working families
- Housing assistance programs
- Consumer affairs and advice
- Landlord and tenant rights
- Child immunization programs and requirements for school attendance
- Traffic laws and violations

- Legal rights in special situations (for example, the right to request an interpreter)
- Location of and joining local libraries
- Recreational opportunities, such as no-fee family days at local museums, zoos, and parks
- Tax information
- Financial literacy: paying bills, finance management, and so forth
- Education and training opportunities
- After-school and vacation programs for children

To keep informed of community issues, instructors can do the following:

- Establish regular contact with key informants from the local county health department, school districts, community-based organizations, department of social services, and consumer affairs and employment rights groups. Encourage them to use the adult education program as a conduit to the language-learning community.
- Maintain a regular program of classroom presentations and information-sharing sessions with supporting content written into the ESL curriculum.
- Create a regular time during instruction for learners to raise hot topics: community-related news, issues, or experiences that can be treated as content for language and literacy instruction.
- Share information at staff meetings about events and situations that may affect learners, and share ideas for using these events as the basis for instruction. Plan collaborative projects around these ideas. (See Moss & Van Duzer, 1998, for how to plan projects for adult ESL classes.)

Identifying the Outcomes Required by Funding Agencies

Funding agencies may or may not stipulate program content. Support from foundations and other private funding organizations may be tied to literacy skills, math skills, or other outcomes, or may be connected with specific instructional methods such as computer-assisted language learning. These requirements will affect the content and instructional approaches adopted by instructors in adult ESL programs.

Federally Funded Programs

As noted in Section 1, Title II of the Workforce Investment Act (WIA) of 1998, the Adult Education and Family Literacy Act (AEFLA), authorizes federal funding for adult education programs. The act establishes three goals for language and literacy instruction:

1. To assist adults in becoming literate and obtaining the knowledge and skills necessary for employment and self-sufficiency
2. To assist parents in obtaining the educational skills needed to become full partners in the educational development of their children
3. To assist adults in completing high school or the equivalent

Any ESL classroom that benefits from federal adult education funding must take account of these three goals as well as the NRS level descriptors (see Figure 1.3) when planning content and choosing instructional approaches.

Accountability requirements under the WIA are tied to statistical information on learning gains and level movements. In order for this information to have comparative value and meaning, the gains and levels that are reported need to be standardized. This generally means using standardized tests that are designed to measure the achievement, knowledge, and skills of large groups of learners across programs. The state funding agencies that distribute the federal funds ask instructors to provide convincing answers to critical questions, such as "Are the students learning what you're teaching?" "How can you prove it?"

From the perspective of funding agencies, standardized tests have the following advantages (Burt & Keenan, 1995; Wrigley, 1992):

- Their construct validity and scoring reliability have been tested.
- They are cost-effective, and many do not require a great deal of training to administer.
- They allow for comparisons across programs.
- Compared to other programs, they can give instructors and learners a better sense of how they are doing.

When funding agencies require standardized tests, instructors include the baseline data gathering as part of the initial needs assessment, use the information in designing instruction, and provide on-going and post-instruction assessments to meet the requirements.

Using Needs Assessment Results

After gathering data through the needs assessment process, instructors must reconcile the agendas of the funders, the program, and the learners. Many adult English language learners can articulate their reasons for coming to instructional programs. These reasons, however, may be highly individual and may not coincide with the agendas mandated by external stakeholders. Section 3 presents strategies for reconciling these agendas in a way that is respectful to the learners who are striving to improve their language skills for application in a variety of workplace and community settings.

SECTION THREE

Reconciling the Agendas

Instructional programs typically identify course content within a framework that specifies context, instructional practices, activities, resources, and materials. In a participatory framework, the curriculum emerges as learners and instructors engage in activities designed to elicit issues of interest that then become the focus of the class. Within other frameworks, the general parameters of curricula might be pre-established based on prior needs assessments. One common curriculum framework is competency-based. This curriculum includes both language skills and content competencies in areas important to adult learners' who want to participate successfully in the community and the workplace. It can also include competencies that reflect the program's response to the agendas mandated by business (SCANS), the federal government (NRS), state and local policies and regulations, and the learners. The requirements and needs of the various stakeholders can be reconciled through content selection and instructional practice.

Reconciling Agendas Through Content Selection

Instructors present the content areas mandated by external stakeholders to learners, inviting them to connect these agendas with their own language needs and learning goals. One program that does this is the Arlington Education and Employment Program (REEP) in Virginia. Instructors involve learners in a "Getting Started" unit in which the learners identify their reasons for studying English and negotiate the curriculum. The REEP curriculum uses a competency-based approach to teaching, providing the life-skills context in which language practice takes place. Each instructional level in the REEP curriculum specifies more topic units than can be covered during a 12-week cycle of 10 to 15 hours of instruction per week. Through the "Getting Started" needs assessment process, learners in each class select four or five topic units that are current priorities for them. The selected units then become the context through which the language skills for that instructional level are taught (Arlington Education and Employment Program, 1994).

The range of topics offered to the learners is determined by the different factors that define what adult English language learners need to know in that particular community, but the learners themselves identify the issues of most pressing concern to them for the current instructional cycle. In this way, the instructor is able to blend the agendas of outside stakeholders with those of the adult learners. This process gives learners a voice in their instruction, informs and shapes teaching, and improves instructional practice by allowing teachers to tailor instruction to the larger set of interests and needs represented within a class.

Reconciling Agendas Through Individual Goal Setting

Working with individual learners to set specific goals provides further opportunities for instructors to connect learners' objectives with external agendas while respecting adults' reasons for seeking language instruction. Individual goal setting also increases learners' motivation and confidence. A 1999 study conducted by the National Center for the Study of Adult Learning and Literacy (NCSALL) sought to identify issues that affect adult learners. The study found that "participants who have goals in mind are likely to persist in their studies, and changing a goal through experience appears to be a positive decision" (Comings, Parrella, & Soricone, 1999, p. 2).

Including individual goal setting as an integral part of the instructional program also provides a way to document gains that are not reflected on standardized tests. This strategy provides ready material for the adult education field when instructors need to articulate the impact of education on the lives of adult learners.

Again, REEP provides a model. The following instructional objectives are established to facilitate individual short-term goal work.

The learners will be able to

1. understand the concept of goal setting;
2. state a realistic goal for the instructional cycle;
3. identify strategies to achieve the goal;
4. create a plan to achieve the goal;
5. carry out the plan, monitor goal work, and refine goals and strategies as needed; and
6. evaluate and demonstrate progress toward or achievement of the goal.

Figure 3.1.
Instructional Process for Individual Short-Term Goal Work

Beginning ➡ ➡	**➡ Ongoing ➡**	**➡ ➡ End**
1. Assessing class needs 2. Identifying and articulating individual goals 3. Planning	4. Carrying out the plan (learners and teachers monitor progress; learner-teacher conference midway)	5. Evaluating and documenting progress (teacher and learner assess goal work; learner-teacher conference)

From *Assessing Individual Learner Goal Achievement* by S. Grant and D. Moss, 2000, Vancouver, British Columbia, Canada: TESOL. Adapted with permission.

These objectives, as well as the student's progress made toward achieving the identified goal, are assessed at the end of the goal process.

At REEP, the instructional process used for individual short-term goal work consists of three phases (Figure 3.1).

Beginning

1. Assessing class needs.

The class needs-assessment or content-selection process identifies the needs and priorities of individual learners as well as the class as a whole. In the class needs-assessment stage, the instructor uses level-appropriate tools to help learners identify their long-term goals and reasons for studying English, identify and prioritize language-skill needs, and select topic units to be covered as a class. If possible, individual goal work should be linked to the learner's long-term goal(s), since successful short-term goals are often components of longer term goals.

When students identify an individual goal within the context of the instructional units that have been selected by the class, the connection between individual and class work is achieved. This activity also helps the instructor to respond to and manage multiple learners' goals.

2. Identifying and articulating individual goals.

Next, the instructor focuses the learners' attention on individual goals that can be accomplished during the time frame designated for the process. The instructor can facilitate the transition from class needs assessment to individual goal articulation by asking students these questions:

- Why are you studying English?
- Which language skill did you choose in the class needs assessment (listening, speaking, reading, writing)? Why is this skill important for you?
- When is this skill difficult for you? Think of a time when you couldn't do something in English.
- What do you want to be able to do when you finish this class?

The goals need to be realistic, measurable, and achievable within the given time frame. Below are some examples of realistic goals articulated by REEP students.

- I need to improve my writing so that I can write letters to my daughter's teachers.
- I need to describe symptoms to the doctor.
- I want to improve my listening so that I can understand TV news programs better.
- I need to practice speaking so I can have a job interview.

If the goals are not realistic and achievable, learners will be frustrated by the process and will not have the sense of accomplishment or progress that motivates them to keep working on their individual goals. Unrealistic goals tend to be too broad, have more than one goal embedded into them, lack focus, have no criteria or context, or lack qualifiers. The following are some examples of unrealistic goals:

- Learn English. (Too broad)
- Improve my pronunciation. (Lacks focus, needs criteria and context)
- Practice speaking. (Lacks focus)

Providing and modeling examples are critical in helping learners articulate realistic goals. The instructor and learners can brainstorm a list of possible goals within a particular context (e.g., family literacy or workforce preparation). Then, using a realistic goal as a sample, the teacher can work with the class to model the process: state the goal, make a pre-assessment, and develop a list of strategies for goal achievement.

Figure 3.2 shows how a group assessment of needs within a narrowly defined content area can be used as the basis for identifying individual goals. The group brainstorms a list of related needs (in this case, using the telephone).

Figure 3.2
Sample Learner Self-Assessment Questionnaire: *Using the Telephone*

Using the Telephone	***It is easy for me.***	***It is OK for me.***	***It is difficult for me.***	***I can't do it.***
Call about an emergency	✔			
Get information about a job				✔
Make a doctor's appointment			✔	
Order pizza, taxi, tickets			✔	
Get information about education				
Talk to the bank about my balance				
Call my child's school				
Understand marketing calls				
Leave messages with people				
Leave messages on machines				
Call the weather number				
Get information				

The list is made into a questionnaire that each learner completes individually. The tally of results for the entire class can be used to inform overall instruction. Additionally, students assess themselves with regard to each task and choose the most important or troublesome task to work on as an individual short-term goal.

After choosing their individual short-term goals, learners write them down. Using a formula for the goal statement can further help learners identify measurable language goals that can be achieved in a given time frame. The goal statements should include *what* (identified skill) and *why* (in order to/so that I can): I need to improve/practice my (skill) in order to (do something). For example,

- "I need to improve my reading so that I can read cookbooks." (Student's long-term goal is to be a chef.)
- "I need to improve my speaking so that I can ask questions in the supermarket."

3. Planning.
At this time, learners plan their strategies. They complete a goal pre-assessment form (such as the one shown in Figure 3.2) that asks them to describe where they are now with their language skills and where they want to be. This assessment serves as a baseline against which to measure progress made throughout the goal process. Even if the goals are not achieved, measuring against the pre-assessment will help the learner to see forward movement. Measuring also helps the learner and the instructor recognize goals that may be too broad for the given time frame or the learner's current abilities.

The instructor reviews the self-assessments, goals, and plans. Learners can also ask peers to help them identify goals that seem unrealistic or plans that do not match the goal. The following questions are helpful during the planning phase:

- Can this goal really be accomplished in the instructional cycle or time period available?
- How will the strategies in the plan help me to achieve my goal?

Worksheets 3.1, 3.2, and 3.3 are models for the goal-identification and planning phases.

WORKSHEET 3.1

GOAL WORKSHEET: Beginning/Intermediate Level

***What Do I Want to Learn?* (12-week goal)**

Name: ______________________________ Date: ______________

I need to improve my ______________________________,

so I can ______________________________.

Now it is (circle one)

very difficult. difficult. so-so. easy.

How will I learn?

I will______________________________.

What did I do?

Date	*What I did*	*It was*	*Comments*
		It was ___ *very difficult* ___ *difficult* ___ *so-so* ___ *easy*	
		___ *very difficult* ___ *difficult* ___ *so-so* ___ *easy*	
		___ *very difficult* ___ *difficult* ___ *so-so* ___ *easy*	
		___ *very difficult* ___ *difficult* ___ *so-so* ___ *easy*	

WORKSHEET 3.2

GOAL WORKSHEET: Beginning/Intermediate Level

My Plan for My Goal

Name: ______________________________ Date: __________

What is my goal? ______________________________

When will I finish?______________________________

Now (circle one)

I can't do it. it is difficult. it is OK. it is easy.

How can I practice?

1.______________________________

2.______________________________

What did I do?

Date	*How I practiced*	*It was* ___ *very difficult* ___ *difficult* ___ *so-so* ___ *easy*	*Comments*
		___ *very difficult* ___ *difficult* ___ *so-so* ___ *easy*	
		___ *very difficult* ___ *difficult* ___ *so-so* ___ *easy*	
		___ *very difficult* ___ *difficult* ___ *so-so* ___ *easy*	

WORKSHEET 3.3

GOAL WORKSHEET: Intermediate/Advanced Level

Learning Contract

Name: ______________________________ Date: ____________

When you finish this English class, what do you want to be able to do with English outside of class?

This plan begins ____________________ and ends ____________________.

My goal is ____,

so that I can ____.

At this time, (circle one)

I can't do it. it's difficult. it's OK. it's easy.

I am going to achieve my goal by doing

1. ____
2. ____
3. ____
4. ____

I am going to show evidence of achievement by

____

____.

Signature: ______________________________ Date: ____________

I can't do it. It's difficult. It's OK. It's easy.

The evidence is ____.

Signature: ______________________________ Date: ____________

Hours of Instruction: __________

Ongoing

4. Carrying out the plan.

Throughout the goal identification process, learners reflect on their progress and activities in different ways, depending on their goals, plans, and learning styles. Some learners enjoy keeping a record of their goal activities in a log or portfolio while others resist these approaches. Most learners enjoy and benefit from opportunities to share their progress with each other and to get feedback from other learners on their progress and strategies. This can be done as a class, in homogenous small groups (learners with similar goals), or heterogeneous small groups (learners with different goals). Most learners also want to talk with and get feedback from their instructors. This can be accomplished during the progress conferences at the middle and end of the teaching cycle. Worksheets 3.4 and 3.5 are examples of how to document progress toward goal attainment.

Practice grid questions with learners before asking them to use the Information Grid Activity (Worksheet 3.5) to monitor goal attainment. The boxes can contain complete questions or cue phrases. Learners can interview each other and record answers on the grid, or the teacher can interview learners and record responses on an overhead transparency of the grid. The class can then analyze the results with the instructor.

End

5. Evaluating and documenting progress.

The learner and the instructor assess progress at the end of the goal process. Learners reflect on their progress toward goal achievement and record their assessment on their goal worksheets. Evidence of progress may include demonstration of new skills; documentation from outside sources (e.g., a promotion or a certificate); statements about how the student feels or functions now; or anecdotal statements such as, "I spoke to my boss about __________. I couldn't do that before."

For an individual goal identified within a specific unit (e.g., a telephone/communications unit), a beginning-level student can complete a basic evaluation form (Worksheet 3.6), which can be used for assessment in any content area. Intermediate- to advanced-level students can complete a form similar to Worksheet 3.7.

The instructor assesses progress toward goal achievement based on overall progress in the class, performance evaluation or student demonstration, learner self-assessment, or achievement of related class objectives. The instructor then records the assessment and evidence on the learner's progress report (Worksheet 3.8). The instructor also assesses achievement of the instructional objectives related to the goal-setting process (Figure 3.1), records the assessment on the learner's progress report, and discusses the progress made during the learner-teacher conference at the end of the cycle.

WORKSHEET 3.4

GOAL MONITORING: Intermediate

Progress on My Short-Term Goal

Name: ______________________________ Date: ______________

Look over the personal goal you made at the beginning of the cycle. Then answer the questions.

My goal: ______________________________

1. In what ways have you been practicing in and outside of class to reach your goal? Give two or more examples of strategies you are using.
   (a) ______________________________
   (b) ______________________________
   (c) ______________________________

2. Approximately how much time per week do you practice your goal outside of class? Is this enough time?

____

3. Circle one of the statements to complete the following sentence:
   Since the beginning of the cycle, I have been making _______ progress toward my goal.
   a lot of   some   very little

4. Do you have any questions for your classmates or your teacher about how to get more practice related to your goal?

____

WORKSHEET 3.5

GOAL MONITORING: Beginning Through Advanced Levels			
Information Grid Activity			
Name	*What is your goal?*	*Are you making progress toward you goal? Give an example.*	*What can you do outside of class to help you achieve you goal?*

WORKSHEET 3.6

GOAL ASSESSMENT: Beginning Level

Goal Assessment

Name: ______________________________ Date: ____________

My goal: ____

How am I doing?

It is easier for me because ___________________________

____

____.

It is still difficult for me because ____________________

____

____.

WORKSHEET 3.7

GOAL ASSESSMENT: Intermediate/Advanced Level

Final Evaluation of a Personal Short-Term Goal

Name: ______________________________________ Date: ______________

Look over the initial goal you set and the progress worksheet you completed mid-cycle. Then, answer the questions below.

1. Did you reach you goal? Yes No

If you checked "yes" for Question 1, answer Questions 2 and 4. If you checked "no" for Question 1, answer Questions 3 and 4.

2. How do you know you achieved your goal? What types of practice helped you most?

____

____

3. Why do you feel you didn't reach your goal? Do you think the goal was realistic?

____

____

4. Do you think the process of setting a goal, monitoring progress, and evaluating it at the end of the cycle was useful? Do you have any suggestions about how the process could be improved in the future?

____

____

WORKSHEET 3.8

PROGRESS REPORT

Goal Process

Name: ______________________________________ Date: __________

+ = achieved
• = needs more practice
A = absent

1. ______ Understands goal setting
2. ______ Identifies a realistic goal
3. ______ Develops a plan
4. ______ Works on plan
5. ______ Evaluates progress

Worksheets 3.1 – 3.8 are from workshops presented by Arlington Education and Employment Program (REEP), 1999-2000, Arlington, VA: Arlington County Public Schools. Adapted with permission.

Figure 3.3 outlines a variety of assessment methods that can be used during the goal-setting process.

Figure 3.3
Assessment Methods for Learning Goals

Assessment Method	Time Period	Description
Interviews	At intake	Staff hold one-on-one conversations with learners to discuss needs, expectations, and reasons for entering an educational program. Long- and short-term goals can be discussed.
Teacher/Learner Conferences	Monitoring phase Evaluation phase	Teacher meets with individual learners to discuss progress being made and next steps.
Teacher Observations and Assessment of Related Objectives	Ongoing	Teacher observes learner's performance of classroom tasks related to objectives, use and management of materials, and interaction with other learners.
Presentations	Evaluation phase	Learner demonstrates knowledge and skills through formal presentation such as teaching others or giving a speech.
Portfolios	Ongoing	Learner collects and saves materials that demonstrate progress toward goal. Examples include writing samples, certificates received, video and audiotapes of performances, and projects completed.
Logs/Journals	Ongoing	Learner keeps a record of activities and work or community accomplishments related to goal, reflecting on progress toward goal. Examples include reading logs, news logs, and dialogue journals.
Outside Documentation	Ongoing	Learner brings to class evidence of progress toward goal. Examples include work certificates, driver's permit or license, notes to child's school, and letters.
Learner Self-Assessment	Ongoing	Learner evaluates achievement of progress toward goal.

From *The REEP Curriculum: A Learner-Centered ESL Curriculum for Adults*, by Arlington Education and Employment Program (REEP), 1994, Arlington, VA: Arlington County Public Schools. Adapted with permission.

Reconciling Agendas Through Instructional Practice

By incorporating needs assessment and goal setting into instruction, instructors are not only identifying the content learners see as priorities, but they are also providing opportunities for learners to develop the skills needed in the workplace and the community. For example, the EFF Standard on "Planning" states that adults need to be able to set and prioritize goals, develop an organized approach to activities and objectives, actively carry out the plan, monitor the plan's progress, and evaluate its effectiveness while considering any need to adjust the plan (Stein, 2000). In the SCANS Three-Part Foundation of Basic Skills and Personal Qualities (Figure 1.1), "Thinking Skills" includes demonstrating proficiency in decision-making, specifying goals and constraints, generating alternatives, considering risks, and evaluating and choosing best alternatives. "Personal Qualities" include demonstrating self-management, setting personal goals, monitoring progress, and exhibiting self-control. These are the skills that learners practice as they identify needs and set goals.

Instructors can reconcile the different agendas of the respective stakeholders and make them mutually supportive by demonstrating the transferability of skills and providing a variety of contexts in which to practice them. For example, in a class working on "speaking up at staff meetings" (identified as a need by an employer), the instructor designs role-plays for speaking up at PTA meetings (for learners whose goal is to participate in their child's education) or community association meetings (for those who want to be proactive in neighborhood issues).

Project-based learning and cooperative learning are other instructional practices that enable the instructor to blend the agendas of multiple stakeholders. These are explained in detail in Sections 4 and 5.

Using Program Management Strategies to Respond to Stakeholder Agendas

Historically, adult education programs have been characterized by an open-enrollment structure (often called *open entry/open exit* or *open-entry*) that responds to the challenges that adult learners face and the mobile nature of their lives. Open enrollment allows learners to enroll and attend as they can, leaving and returning to programs as their life situations permit. However, an open-entry system prevents programs from gathering the data they need to report quantifiable learning outcomes. In addition, adult learners themselves have expressed concern that this system adversely affects their ability to achieve their learning goals (Sticht, 1999).

At Mount Diablo Adult Education in Contra Costa County, California, program administrators held a student focus group to solicit input on the program and specifically on the open-enrollment intake practice (P. Norgaard, personal communication, 2000). The following questions were posed to the group:

- What are some of the reasons you are studying English?
- What are some things you like most about the ESL program?
- Are there any things you do not like about the ESL program?
- Do you like to take tests? Why or why not?
- Do you know what you have to do to be promoted to the next level?
- Why do you choose to attend class in the morning (or afternoon or evening)?
- How often do you attend class?
- What would make you attend class more often?
- Should students be dropped if they don't attend often? How many absences should be allowed?
- Do you like open enrollment? Why or why not?

Overall, the students demonstrated a serious commitment to the instructional program through requests for

- a strict attendance policy with students dropped after just a few absences;
- a structured program with a beginning and an end and clear and accessible criteria for level completion and promotion;
- tests to help them assess their own progress;
- minimizing disruptions to the instructional flow caused by new students continually joining the class; and
- a course of instruction less than 18 weeks. (Students indicated that they could commit to regular attendance if the terms were shorter.)

After reviewing student responses, program managers at Mount Diablo Adult Education realized that they could both support their students and improve their chances of producing measurable outcomes for program funders and other stakeholders by making the following changes:

- Shift from 18-week semesters to trimesters of 14, 12, and 11 weeks.
- Refocus on identifying students' goals and ensuring curricular relevance.
- Identify and emphasize curriculum essentials.
- Focus on identifying assessments before choosing lessons and activities; assess more routinely and effectively.
- Raise expectations for student attendance and participation.
- Limit the number of days and hours available for new student registration.
- At the beginning of each trimester, consolidate students who are continuing at the same instructional level into classes that do not receive new placements. Place new students in their own class.

Discussions and plans for the future of Mount Diable Adult Education include

- using detailed certificates for level completion,
- limiting the days and hours available for new student registration,
- using more internally standardized/shared assessments, and
- creating an orientation class to receive new students or the creation of a video for new students to explain program procedures and expectations.

These practices represent a program management approach to meeting the needs of multiple stakeholders. Adult learners appreciate and prefer more structured programs where entry, exit, and promotion criteria are clear and the class population does not change on a daily basis. When retention improves, programs are better able to produce paired-assessment data based on both pre- and post-measures—a necessary prerequisite for demonstrating learning gains to funders, lawmakers, and other service providers.

Section 4 discusses ways that instructional process and content can help prepare learners to be successful in the workplace and in the wider community.

SECTION FOUR

Conveying Workplace and Civics Competencies Through Instructional Process and Content

Helping adult learners of English achieve their individual goals while acquiring the knowledge and skills they need to succeed in the workplace and the community does not require reinventing the curriculum. The competencies outlined by EFF and SCANS are a combination of basic communication skills and interpersonal and higher order thinking skills that form a part of any adult education curriculum. Whether adult learners are enrolled in mainstream ESL classes or employment-specific programs, these skills frequently form the core of existing curricular content. The workplace competencies that build on these skills can be incorporated into instruction through choices in teaching methodology.

Workplace and Civics Competencies and Instructional Process

Recognizing the Process-Oriented Nature of EFF and SCANS

The workplace and civics competencies that make up EFF do not define content knowledge (what people know) but rather process knowledge (what people do and how they do it). The SCANS competencies, though organized somewhat differently, have a similar focus. A comparison of the two systems, as seen in Figure 4.1, makes this clear.

The most direct way for instructors to help learners develop these skills is to create a classroom environment that simulates real-life situations. As learners are expected to take active roles in the workplace and the community, so they can be encouraged to take active roles in the learning process.

This approach to classroom instruction can build on existing curricular content, especially content that learners have indicated as most important to them. For example, when learners have identified *talking and reading about foods* as an interest, the instructor can incorporate workplace skills into a unit on food. Language instruction might focus on food-related vocabulary, the grammatical structure of comparative and superlative statements, and the use of language functions for expressing preferences about food. Concurrently, the learners develop these language skills within the real-life context of making a budget and comparing prices of food items at different supermarkets in order to plan a reception or large party.

Figure 4.1.
EFF Standards and SCANS Competencies

EFF Standards	SCANS Competencies
Communication Skills	
Reading – Determine purpose, select strategies, monitor comprehension, analyze and integrate information	*Basic Skills* – Read, write, do math, listen, speak, interpret, organize information and ideas
Writing – Determine purpose, organize and present information, use language correctly and appropriately, revise	*Thinking Skills* – Think creatively, make decisions, solve problems, visualize, know how to learn and reason
Speaking – Determine purpose, organize information, use language correctly and appropriately, monitor effectiveness	
Listening – Attend, use appropriate strategies, monitor comprehension, integrate new information with prior knowledge	*Personal Qualities* – Responsibility, self-esteem, sociability, self-management, integrity, honesty
Observing – Attend, use appropriate strategies, monitor comprehension, analyze and integrate information	
Decision-Making Skills	
Math – Understand and work with symbolic information, apply math to solve problems, select data, use symbols to communicate	*Resource Management* – Identify, organize, plan, and allocate time, money, materials, staff
Problems and Decisions – Anticipate problems, understand causes, identify and evaluate solutions, establish criteria for solution selection	
Planning – Set and prioritize goals, develop organized approach, carry out and monitor plan, evaluate effectiveness	
Interpersonal Skills	
Cooperate – Interact courteously and respectfully, seek and give input, adjust actions to others' needs and group goals	*Interpersonal Skills* – Work on teams, teach others, serve customers, lead, negotiate, work in culturally diverse settings
Advocate and Influence – Define goals, gather supporting information, make a case, revise	*Information Management* – Acquire and evaluate facts, organize and maintain data, interpret and communicate information, use computers
Conflict Resolution – Identify areas of agreement/disagreement, generate win/win options, engage parties in negotiation, evaluate and revise approach	
Guide Others – Assess others' needs and own ability, use appropriate strategies, build on others' strengths	
Lifelong Learning Skills	
Responsibility – Establish goals, identify own strengths/weaknesses, employ range of strategies, monitor progress, test in real life	*Systems* – Understand social, organizational, and technological systems, monitor and correct performance, improve/design systems
Reflect and Evaluate – Assess extent and relevance of current knowledge, make inferences, predictions, judgments	*Technology* – Select appropriate technology, apply technology to tasks, maintain and troubleshoot equipment
Research – Pose questions, use multiple lines of inquiry, organize/analyze findings	
Technology – Use electronic tools to acquire, process, and manage information and practice skills	

From *EFF Content Standards for Adult Literacy and Lifelong Learning*, by National Institute for Literacy, 2000, Washington, DC: Author. Available: http://www.nifl.gov/lincs/collections/eff/standards/eff_standards_text.html

From *What Work Requires of Schools*, by Secretary's Commission on Achieving Necessary Skills, 1991, Washington, DC: U.S. Department of Labor. Available: http://wdr.doleta.gov/SCANS/whatwork/whatwork.html

Inherent in this real-life context are a number of workplace and civics competencies. When learners determine how much their budget will cover, they are making decisions and allocating resources (EFF decision-making skills: problems and decisions; SCANS resource management competency). When they compare food prices at different stores, they are acquiring and organizing information and using math to calculate (EFF decision-making skills: math; SCANS information management competency). When they plan the reception, including selecting and reserving a location and developing a timetable for setup and cleanup, learners are developing an organized approach, evaluating alternatives, and anticipating problems (EFF decision-making skills: planning; SCANS systems competency). They are also working as part of a team and negotiating (EFF and SCANS interpersonal skills).

By using learner-identified issues as the context for language instruction and as the vehicle for practicing workplace and civics competencies, instructors can respond to a variety of stakeholder agendas at the same time. Similarly, essential or program-mandated content material can also be used to respond to learner-identified language and literacy goals. For example, an employment-focused class can demonstrate its responsiveness to learners' needs by presenting the mandated content material in a way that emphasizes the speaking or writing skills learners have labeled as most important.

Using Learner-Centered Instruction

When instructional practices emphasize learner interaction and responsibility for the learning process, instructors are responding to multiple stakeholder agendas. In learner-centered instruction, the teacher encourages learners to learn independently and from one another and coaches them in the skills they need to do so efficiently. The teacher's role is that of learning facilitator, and learners are actively engaged in learning rather than just passively listening to the teacher.

Many of the processes and methods currently used in ESL instruction employ learner-centered strategies that contribute to the development of workplace and civics competencies. Cooperative learning activities give learners opportunities to interact with others, seek and offer input, advocate and influence, negotiate, and teach others while they are learning language. Project assignments, whether given to individuals or to small groups, provide opportunities for students to learn through research, to organize and interpret information, and to communicate it with others. Students can use technology (e.g., Internet, word processing, videos) to research and present their projects. In these activities, learners develop the information management and technology competencies as well as the interpersonal skills identified by both SCANS and EFF as necessary for success.

Learner-centered instruction also encourages students to develop the lifelong learning skills outlined in the EFF Standards and relevant SCANS Competencies. It prepares learners for the workplace, as well as for civics and family responsibilities, providing a model for how to learn independently, from coworkers, and from other community members. Learner-centered instruction may take a variety of forms, some of which are outlined below.

Information gathering and reporting activities.
Learners collect and organize specified information, which they then analyze and evaluate. They may report in teams or individually on the information they have gathered, presenting it graphically, orally, or in writing (EFF and SCANS communication and interpersonal skills).

Example A: *Give One and Get One*

1. Learners individually list three to five items related to the assigned topic. For example, if learners have been practicing ways to ask for clarification, they list three to five phrases they can use to check their understanding (e.g., "Could you repeat that please?" "Do you mean _________ or _________?" "I'm sorry, I don't understand." "Did you say _________?")

2. Working within a time frame established by the instructor, each learner talks to three classmates, one at a time. The two compare lists and ask questions about new or confusing items, then select one item from the other's list to add to their own.

3. Volunteers report newly learned information to the class: "I found out from _________ that _________. "_________ told me that _________."

Example B: *Surveys*

Learner-conducted surveys are an excellent way to invite independent interaction in the classroom, both in information gathering and in presentation and reporting. For example, a simple survey idea is "Who are you and where are you from?"

1. Learners interview their classmates to learn names, the spelling of first and last names, countries of origin, and the spelling of the country names.
2. Learners record the information they have gathered in a table: last name, first name, and country of origin.
3. Learners tally the figures, listing the countries represented and the number of learners from each country.
4. Learners create a graphic, such as a bar graph or pie chart, to present the information in the tally.

Example C: *Diagrams*

This diagram was created by a group of low-level Hmong ESL learners who had limited literacy skills in both Hmong and English. The learners practiced the target language by asking and answering the questions "How did you go to Thailand?" and "When did you go to Thailand?" They then conducted a survey using these questions and organized and presented the information they had collected. Despite their limited literacy skills, the learners were able to demonstrate effective competency in communication, planning, cooperating with others, and learning through research.

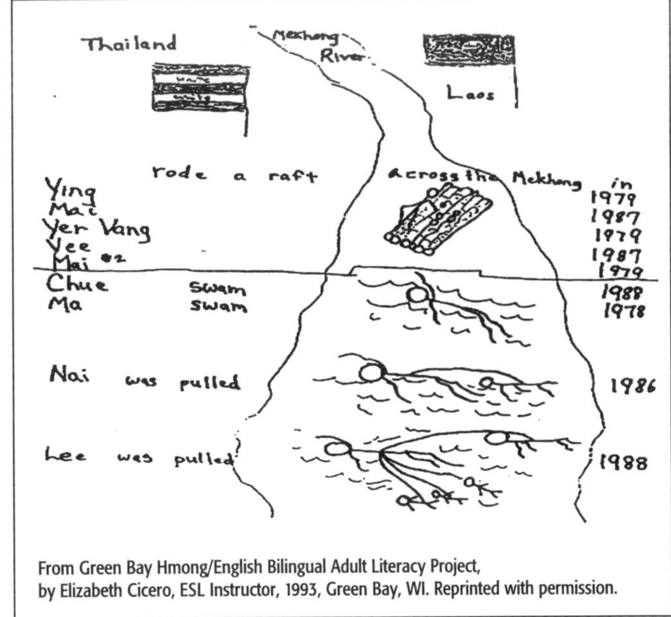

From Green Bay Hmong/English Bilingual Adult Literacy Project, by Elizabeth Cicero, ESL Instructor, 1993, Green Bay, WI. Reprinted with permission.

Cooperative learning.

In cooperative learning activities, learners work and learn together in groups of two to five. Cooperative learning, however, is more than simply having learners work together in groups. Activities are designed so each group member plays a specific role to complete a group task. Cooperative learning provides opportunities for learners to develop decision-making, problem-solving, and interpersonal skills identified by EFF and SCANS (see Figure 4.1).

Jigsaw activities practice cooperative learning skills by requiring students to learn new information and teach it to others. Jigsaws can be set up in a variety of ways. The following instructions outline the basic concept of a jigsaw activity.

1. Learners number off in "home" teams, one through four.
2. All learners with the same number regroup to form "expert" teams.
3. Each expert team studies a specified segment of information.
4. Home teams come together again. Learners teach each other the segment of information they have learned in their expert teams or contribute their knowledge to completion of a team project.

Jigsaws can be used with learners at all levels. The following guidelines (Wislofsky, n.d.) offer suggestions for jigsaw reading activities to use with beginning-level learners .

1. Choose reading passages with previously learned vocabulary so that learners will be familiar with the words. A jigsaw reading is good to do at the end of a unit.
2. If possible, provide visuals to assist with comprehension of the material.
3. Divide the reading into two or three parts. Then organize learners to work in pairs on each portion of the text. For example, if a reading is divided into three parts, the home team should consist of six people (three pairs). Portions of the text can be color-coded to assist group formation.
4. Model one complete lesson with the whole class, carefully taking learners through each step.
5. Focus learners on the important parts of their passages—the key information that they will be sharing.
6. Give learners ample time to rehearse what they will teach to the members of their home team about their passage.

Note: A jigsaw reading exercise works best if it can be completed in one instructional session.

If learners are already familiar with working in groups or in a cooperative learning environment, the following activities will help strengthen interpersonal skills needed for cooperative learning. (See Bell, 1988, for more cooperative learning activities to use with ESL learners.)

Numbered Heads Together

1. Learners number off in teams, one through four.
2. The teacher asks a question.
3. Each team discusses possible answers for a specified amount of time.
4. The teacher calls a number from one to four, and the learners on each team with that number respond to the question.

Think-Pair-Share

1. Learners individually think about a problem or question raised by the instructor or by a designated learner and write down their ideas.
2. Learners then pair up to compare answers and develop a response that combines their ideas.
3. One member of each pair shares their answer with the class.

Instructional Process and the National Reporting System

Learner-centered instruction provides opportunities for learners to develop and practice the skills outlined in the National Reporting System (NRS) Educational Functional Levels (Figure 1.3) as well as those outlined in the EFF Standards and SCANS Competencies. Although the NRS descriptors are broader and less detailed than EFF or SCANS, like EFF and SCANS, they are life skills and describe what a learner is expected to be able to do. These include such skills as clarifying and following oral and written directions, interpreting charts and graphs, using oral and written English to give and obtain information, and using technology.

Workplace and Civics Competencies and Instructional Content

There are some competencies that are not built into existing curricula and therefore warrant specific content knowledge development. This is true particularly in the case of the personal qualities and interpersonal skills required for workplace success. In the EFF model, a successful worker must "interact with others in ways that are friendly, courteous, and tactful, and that demonstrate respect for others' ideas, opinions, and contributions; seek input from others in order to understand their actions and reactions; offer clear input on own interests and attitudes so others can understand one's actions and reactions; and try to adjust one's actions to take into account the needs of others and/or the task to be accomplished" (Stein, 2000, p. 41). In the SCANS model, the successful worker possesses the "Personal Qualities" of responsibility, self-esteem, sociability, self-management, integrity, and honesty (see Figures 1.1 and 4.1).

Many of these concepts are open to cultural interpretation. However, English language learners living and working in the United States must develop an understanding of the U.S. interpretation of these concepts in order to interact successfully with co-workers and neighbors. Using newspaper working-life advice columns and magazine articles on workplace behavior as the basis for class discussion and other activities is a way to approach these topics in the classroom. Learners can be encouraged to compare and contrast varied points of view as they develop an understanding of the cultural norms of the communities in which they are living and working.

Integrating Workplace Skills Throughout the Instructional Session

Teachers often direct the presentation and review parts of lessons. Learner-centered activities are more easily incorporated into the practice section. However, there are some simple strategies that teachers can use during all parts of an instructional session to provide opportunities for workplace-skill development.

Using Involvement Strategies

Involvement strategies or techniques keep all learners actively engaged in learning throughout the instructional session. These strategies replicate the behavioral expectations of the workplace, where workers are expected to demonstrate personal responsibility by being involved and engaged in their work at all times, not just when the supervisor calls on them.

When checking for comprehension of instructions or when conducting review activities, many instructors ask questions of a class and invite learners to raise their hands to volunteer an answer. An alternative to calling on one learner is to ask *all* learners to answer. For example, instead of asking, "Did Irina accept the job at the garage?" the instructor makes the statement, "Irina accepted the job at the garage." Learners raise their hands if they believe the statement is true or keep their hands down if they believe it is false. This simple instructional strategy establishes the expectation that all learners will be actively involved in responding to the instructor's input.

A similar involvement technique uses number fans (Fellows, 1998). The fans are made from thin strips of cardstock; each strip has a number from 0–5 printed at one end, and the strips are fastened together with a butterfly fastener at the other end. Each learner has a fan. The instructor can ask questions in a multiple-choice format, with the numbers on the fans corresponding to the possible answers. In addition to establishing the expectation of involvement by all learners, this strategy enables the instructor to see, by looking around the room at the displayed numbers, who is able to respond and who is struggling.

Another involvement strategy is to make individual success dependent on structured interaction with other learners so that learners are invested in one another's learning as well as their own. For example, all learners can be required to have work assignments and projects checked by another learner before they are submitted to the instructor. The instructor can create a peer-evaluation form for learners to include with any work they submit (see Worksheets 6.2, 6.3, and 6.4).

Establishing Expectations for Interaction

To encourage learner involvement and interaction, instructors can create an atmosphere where it is safe to ask questions. For example, instructors can replace teacher questions such as "Do you understand?" with open-ended invitations such as "What questions do you have?" or "Who has a question?" To reduce individual learners' anxiety about having their lack of comprehension highlighted, the instructor can emphasize the helpfulness and productivity of asking the question by commending the questioner with positive statements: "Thanks for asking that question." "That's a helpful question." "That question will help everyone."

Instructors also need to model and insist on respectful classroom interactions in which everyone listens when someone is sharing information. Instructors can teach appropriate language for classroom interactions, such as "Could you speak up, please?" and "Excuse me, could you repeat that?" Instructors can also model appropriate body language and explain what is considered inappropriate. This discussion can provide an opportunity for instructor and learners to explore what is considered polite and respectful and relate that to the culture of the U.S. workplace.

Finally, instructors can encourage interaction and involvement by using classroom-management techniques (described in Section 5) to establish the expectation that all learners will take responsibility for the learning that takes place in the classroom.

SECTION FIVE

Conveying Behavior Expectations Through Classroom Management Techniques

Within every society exists a standard of expected behavior, both in the workplace and in the day-to-day interactions with salespeople, health care providers, school personnel, and so forth. With the use of management techniques, instructors can create a classroom environment for English language learners that simulates the behavioral expectations of the U.S. workplace and community.

Classroom management techniques—including rules of behavior, routines, established procedures, room organization and layout, student job assignments, and organization of learners into teams—provide an organizational structure for the learning environment. These techniques teach learners to work within a system and invite them to accept responsibility for their own learning. A classroom that makes learners responsible for their own success models the environment they will encounter in the workplace and the wider community.

Behavioral Expectations in the Workplace and the Community

Standards of workplace behavior include punctuality, responsiveness, accountability, and initiative. These expected behaviors reflect the culture of the United States but may or may not coincide with the learners' understanding of appropriate behavior that they bring from their countries of origin. Allocating class time for discussion of cross-cultural differences and expected behaviors in the United States will help learners develop and practice these patterns of behavior and interaction skills. Another benefit of understanding cultural differences is that increasingly, in the U.S. workplace and community, people are expected to be team players who can communicate and work well with people of diverse backgrounds (Price-Machado, 1996).

Both the EFF Standards and the SCANS Competencies address the interpersonal skills that successful individuals in the United States are expected to possess (Figure 4.1). The classroom management techniques discussed in this section provide ways for instructors to incorporate the practice of these EFF and SCANS skills into the instructional environment in meaningful ways. Rules and routines for student behavior encourage development of the self-management skills that underlie lifelong learning. Classroom rules and procedures also provide opportunities to design, understand, and function successfully within a system. Similarly, team assignments and within-team role assignments enable learners to practice interpersonal skills, use resources and systems effectively, and exercise planning and decision-making skills.

The basic requirement for effective classroom management is for instructors to model good organizational skills, reflecting expected workplace behavior. The instructor arrives on time and comes prepared with an organized instructional plan that is communicated to learners. An effective way to do this is to start each class session with an agenda that can be referred to at various times throughout the session. This draws students' attention to organization and class structure, invites them to reflect on what has been achieved within an allocated time period, and keeps them aware of the fact that they are functioning within a system.

Building Individual Responsibility Through Rules and Routines

Individual responsibility, integrity, and self-management are fundamental to success in the workplace. When workers forget their uniforms, fail to take care of equipment assigned to them, or are unable to account for materials and resources allocated to them, supervisors are unlikely to be sympathetic.

Organizational skills, self-management, appropriate attitude, and personal responsibility can be modeled and practiced through the establishment of routines in the classroom. It may not be obvious to all learners that they must bring papers and pens to class every day or that it makes sense to organize class handouts by topic or date. This is not a question of capability. (Individuals who have fled war-torn countries and maneuvered families to safety or have planned for and negotiated immigration procedures have considerable skills and capabilities.) Rather, it is a matter of knowing and understanding the expectations that govern behavior in the U.S. workplace and communities. To develop learners' understanding while building on their strengths, instructors must establish rules and routines that will enable them to be systematic as they learn and operate effectively within social, professional, and technological systems.

Instructors can create systems in the classroom that set expectations for personal organization, preparedness, and responsibility, and also provide opportunities for learners to document that they are meeting those expectations. For example, learners can be asked to maintain weekly checklists to keep track of what they need to bring to class and tasks they need to complete in class. Those with school-age children can compare their homework charts and checklists with the ones their children bring home from school. In this way, parents can help their children learn as they themselves are learning.

Worksheets 5.1, 5.2, and 5.3 are personal weekly checklists, developed by Judy Rosselli for her intermediate Vocational-ESL (VESL) class in San Diego, California.

WORKSHEET 5.1

Personal Checklist A

Theme: ______________________________

Focus question: ______________________________

Week of: ______________________________

Name: ______________________ Room: __________

Put a check ✔ in the chart for the answers that are true.

	Monday	Tuesday	Wednesday	Thursday	Friday
Arrived on time to class					
Brought papers, notebook, and pencil					
Completed homework					
Worked with other students					
Filled out attendance checklist					

Homework Schedule

Monday: ______________________________

Tuesday: ______________________________

Wednesday: ______________________________

Thursday: ______________________________

Friday: ______________________________

Signature: ______________________ Date: __________

Name (printed): ______________________________

WORKSHEET 5.2

Personal Checklist B

Theme: ______________________________

Focus question: ______________________________

Week of: ______________________________

Name: ______________________________ Room: ______________

Circle a number for each statement below.

Arrived on time to class	Low	1	2	3	4	5	High
Brought papers, notebook, and pencil	Low	1	2	3	4	5	High
Completed homework	Low	1	2	3	4	5	High
Worked with other students	Low	1	2	3	4	5	High
Filled out attendance checklist	Low	1	2	3	4	5	High

Homework Schedule

Monday: ______________________________

Tuesday: ______________________________

Wednesday: ______________________________

Thursday: ______________________________

Friday: ______________________________

Signature: ______________________________ Date: ______________

Name (printed): ______________________________

WORKSHEET 5.3

Weekly Report

Theme: ______________________________

Week of: ______________________________

Name: ______________________________ Room: __________

1. Personal Checklist

Fill in the chart. Use the letter **Y** for yes and the letter **N** for no. If you were absent, use the letter **A**. If it was a holiday, use the letter **H**.

	Monday	Tuesday	Wednesday	Thursday	Friday
I arrived on time to class.					
I called in to class when I was absent.					
I brought papers, notebook, and pencil.					
I worked with other students.					
I filled out my attendance checklist.					
I completed my group task.					
I came back from break on time.					

2. Reflection

My favorite class activity this week was ______________________________

____

The most difficult class activity this week was ______________________________

____

3. Important!

If you cannot come to class, please call ______________ and leave a message.

My name is ______________________. I study in Room __________.

I cannot come to class today.

Name: ______________________________ Date: __________

From the classroom of Judy Roselli. Reprinted with permission.

Generating Involvement and Systems Awareness Through Class Rules and Procedures

The foremost goal of classroom-management should be student responsibility. Involving learners in the establishment of class rules and the definition of procedures ensures the student support or buy-in that is critical to the success of these techniques. Furthermore, creating systems that encourage student responsibility will minimize the amount of time and energy the instructor must expend on activities that distract from facilitating learning.

Simple strategies can give learners control over how a classroom functions and can encourage them to make decisions collaboratively, solve problems, think creatively, and exercise responsibility. Suggestion boxes can yield excellent student input on issues from interpersonal conflicts in the classroom to furniture layout. Instructors and learners can work together to develop a list of classroom jobs and a job-assignment rotation. This procedure may take different forms, depending on the ability level of the class. For example, an instructor at Merced Adult School in California had his beginning-level ESL learners create a mission statement for the class and a set of "opportunities" that teams of learners were asked to take responsibility for during each session.

Mission Statement

Just as a team works together to win, our teams will work together to win the prize of learning English.

Opportunities

1. Pass out papers
2. Pass out dictionaries
3. Collect dictionaries
4. Get water for coffee
5. Clean coffee area
6. Keep books in order
7. Keep desks and chairs in order
8. Train newcomers
9. Answer the telephone

Work Orders

Classroom management techniques invite the instructor to turn classroom challenges into opportunities for learning. For example, if the bulb in the overhead projector burns out, learning will be affected. It makes sense to expect the learners to share responsibility for solving the problem. Procedures can be established for handling such problems, and responsibility for following the procedures can be turned over to the learners.

Judy Rosselli developed such a routine for her VESL office systems preparation class. Because it is dedicated to office-systems instruction, the room has many pieces of equipment that require regular maintenance. Rosselli's routine reduces the amount of time she must take from her most important job—facilitating learning—while providing opportunities for her learners to work within a system, take responsibility for their own learning, practice organizational skills, and identify and troubleshoot problems. Worksheet 5.4 shows the form Rosselli has her students use when equipment needs to be repaired.

Classroom Rules

Instructor and learners can work together to develop standardized classroom procedures and rules for student behavior. Standardized procedures are most effective for regular or on-going activities, such as turning in written assignments, conducting peer reviews, and rotating the use of computers. Rules for behavior may address absence and tardiness, preparation for class, and other matters of individual responsibility. Procedures and rules can be documented and displayed in the classroom, and learners can be asked to accept responsibility for informing newcomers to the class about the procedures and rules. This is especially important in an open-entry class where new learners are continually arriving.

These classroom techniques simulate the operational procedures that many learners will experience in the workplace. They communicate clear expectations for class participation and reduce the amount of organizational work required by the instructor. They also provide learners with valuable opportunities to practice interacting with systems, procedures, written instructions, and policies. This kind of classroom-based training may be the only preparation that some learners have for the expectations they will encounter in the workplace and the community. Additionally, these procedures give learners direct experience with commonly used K-12 classroom activities, enabling them to understand and support their children's education.

WORKSHEET 5.4

VESL Classroom Work Order

FORM 1: Please fill out the following information for the piece of equipment that is in need of repair. Attach this form to the piece of equipment that needs repair and place FORM 2 (below) in the **NEEDS REPAIR** box. Thank you.

Date of Request: ______________________________

Requested By: ______________________________

Type of Equipment: ______________________________

Brand Name and Model: ______________________________

Serial Number: ______________________________

Classroom Number: ______________________________

Description of Problem: ______________________________

____

Signature: ______________________________

FORM 2: Please fill out the following information for the piece of equipment that is in need of repair. Place this form in the **NEEDS REPAIR** box and attach FORM 1 (above) to the piece of equipment that needs repair. Thank you.

Date of Request: ______________________________

Requested By: ______________________________

Type of Equipment: ______________________________

Brand Name and Model: ______________________________

Serial Number: ______________________________

Classroom Number: ______________________________

Description of Problem: ______________________________

____

Signature: ______________________________

From the classroom of Judy Roselli. Reprinted with permission.

Donna Price-Machado established a set of rules with her class of high-intermediate VESL learners at San Diego Community College in California. The rules are connected to a point system in which teams receive or lose points on the basis of team members' behavior. A set of trainer instructions is used by current class members to help newcomers understand the established classroom procedures. Figures 5.1–5.4 show the classroom rules, the trainer instructions, the class routine, and the system for submitting written assignments.

Figure 5.1
Rules for Our VESL Classroom

1. If you are going to be absent, call the teacher at [insert phone number] or tell her in advance. If you don't call, your team will lose one point for that day.
2. You must put all your checklists in a folder and leave the folder in class. Put the folder in alphabetical order behind the letter of your last name in the file cabinet located near the door as you walk into the classroom. DO NOT TAKE YOUR CHECKLISTS HOME.
3. If you will be late to school because of an appointment, tell the teacher or tell a teammate and ask him/her to tell the teacher. You need to communicate with your teacher and teammates.
4. You must come back to class on time after break. If you are late, it is your responsibility to apologize to the class for the disruption.
5. If you need to speak your native language in class for a translation or grammar explanation, you should ask permission from the teacher and the other learners first. Remember that you come to school to practice your English, so it benefits you to speak English as much as you can during the class.
6. Bring your ESL notebook with all of your English papers in it every day. If you forget or lose a paper that your teacher gives you, it is your responsibility to get the sheet from another student and make a copy.
7. Bring a small vocabulary notebook to class with you every day. Write all the new vocabulary words you learn in that small notebook.
8. Write what you learned in class every day in your Blue Book.
9. Every Friday we will have a vocabulary and grammar test covering the material that we have studied during that week.

REMEMBER! Everything you do affects your teammates, just as at work your actions affect your co-workers. If you are late, absent, or uncooperative, your teammates suffer, too.

From the classroom of Donna Price-Machado, VESL Instructor, 1996, San Diego Community College District, CA. Reprinted with permission.

Figure 5.2
Trainer Instructions

After the student reads the "Rules for Our VESL Classroom" sheet, ask the following questions. The correct answers are at the bottom of the page.

1. If you can't come to class, what do you need to do?
2. When can you speak your native language in class?
3. What do you need to do if you forget or lose a paper the teacher gives you?
4. What happens if you come back late from break?
5. What do you have to bring to class every day?
6. What should you do when you learn new vocabulary words?
7. When do you have a vocabulary and grammar test?

ANSWERS

1. Before the class, call and leave a message or write a note and give it to the teacher.
2. When you ask permission from the teacher and the other learners.
3. You have to make a copy for yourself.
4. You have to apologize to the class.
5. An ESL notebook and a small vocabulary notebook.
6. You write the new words in a small notebook. This will help you remember the words, and you can study them easily if they are in one place.
7. Every Friday.

From the classroom of Donna Price-Machado, VESL Instructor, 1996, San Diego Community College District, CA. Reprinted with permission.

Figure 5.3
Intermediate-Level VESL Class Routine

1. Every day we will have a dictation of four sentences. These sentences will cover the grammar that we will study during the week. On Friday there will be a grammar test.
2. Every day we will write new vocabulary words on the board. You must copy these words in your small vocabulary notebook. On Friday you will have a vocabulary test.
3. Everyone should use the computer every day. You can practice typing or do grammar, spelling, vocabulary, or idiom exercises on the computer. REMEMBER! To get an office job you must be able to type 35 words per minute.
4. On Mondays and Wednesdays we will talk about news and current events. You will learn many new vocabulary words on these days. Watch the news and read the newspaper so that you can contribute to the class.

From the classroom of Donna Price-Machado, VESL Instructor, 1996, San Diego Community College District, CA. Reprinted with permission.

Figure 5.4
What Do You Do When You Finish a Written Lesson?

When you are finished doing your written work, you must

1. Put the assignment in the IN tray. Be sure that the work is neat and on a clean piece of paper with your name on it.

After I grade your paper, I will put it in the OUT tray.

The day after you give me the assignment,

2. Go to the OUT tray. Find your paper.
3. If there are mistakes, you must make corrections and then put your work back in the IN tray.
4. If I think there is something that you really don't understand, I will write "SEE ME." I can probably see you during class, but if there are a lot of learners, you must make an appointment by writing your name on the appointment sheet on the board under the time you want.
5. When everything is accurate in your written work, bring me your checklist, and I will check off that lesson/competency. Put your lessons in your three-ring notebook.

From the classroom of Donna Price-Machado, VESL Instructor, 1996, San Diego Community College District, CA. Reprinted with permission.

Using Teamwork to Simulate the Work Environment

The ability to work with others as a contributing member of a team is critical to success in the U.S. workplace. Effective team members are able to define and support viewpoints and needs, consider the views and needs of others, negotiate agreement and resolve divergent interests, and guide or teach others. Establishing teams within the classroom for completion of learning activities and for classroom maintenance tasks provides opportunities for learners to develop these competencies. Teams can be established on a short-term, lesson-by-lesson basis or on a long-term basis.

Long-Term Teams

Establishing long-term teams that have classroom maintenance duties assigned to them for a fixed period of time simulates the dynamics of the workplace. Criteria for grouping learners into teams will vary depending on the makeup of the class and the priorities of the teacher. Instructors may group learners on the basis of mixed language backgrounds, ability levels, or gender groups, or learners may form their own groups. No matter how the groups are formed, interpersonal challenges will exist within them, just as they exist in a workplace team. Managing these conflicts will help build interpersonal skills in the team members. In open-entry classes where there are frequent arrivals and departures, learners can experience a typical workplace situation where crew or team members are expected to train new employees or fill in for absentees.

Organizational Team Charts

Organizational team charts can be used to facilitate the operation of long-term teams in the classroom. Assigning regular duties to all learners in the classroom with tasks organized and rewarded by team creates expectations for high performance from other team members. Learners develop the sense that they are participating both for their own benefit and for that of the team.

Price-Machado uses a highly structured team chart that lays out weekly classroom management responsibilities for each team (Figure 5.5). Integral to this classroom management technique is the need to have current class members involved in training newcomers in the teamwork system. Price-Machado has developed a student letter that is given to all newcomers (Figure 5.6) and a set of instructions for the team of trainers to use when teaching newcomers how the team chart works (Figure 5.7).

Figure 5.5
Teamwork Chart

Team & Job	Monday	Tuesday	Wednesday	Thursday	Friday	Notes	Weekly Totals
#1 Erase board. Help teacher with equipment	***Hector*** job: 2 att:: 2	***Sara*** job: 2 att:: 2	***Kidan*** job: 1 att:: 2	***Cruz*** job: 0 att:: 1	***Vankeo*** job: 2 att:: 2	-2 Cruz didn't call–job done by team member -1 Kidan didn't erase board	**17**
#2 Turn off computers and screens	job: att::	job: att::	job: att::	job: att::	job: att::		
#3 Make sure all students sign in; arrange desks	job: att::	job: att::	job: att::	job: att::	job: att::		
#4 Trainers: help teacher with new students	job: att::	job: att::	job: att::	job: att::	job: att::		
#5 Answer phone; take messages	job: att::	job: att::	job: att::	job: att::	job: att::		
#6 Be sure materials are put back	job: att::	job: att::	job: att::	job: att::	job: att::		

HOW THE CHART WORKS:

- The chart is on an erasable poster board. It always hangs in the room and students check their jobs and points daily.
- The team members stay the same for two or three months.
- The team changes jobs every week.
- The teacher adds the points at the end of each week. At the end of the month, the team with the most points wins "The Team of the Month." Their picture is taken and posted. Each member of the winning team is given a small prize, usually a pen or something useful in class.

Rules: Using team #1 above as an example.

Job. There are two points possible for job. On Monday, Hector must erase the board and help with the overhead projector. He must watch and take the initiative to do this; students can ask if the instructor is ready. If Hector is absent on his job day, other students in his team must cover for him to get the points.

Att. = Attendance. To receive the two points for that day for Attendence, everyone must be present. If someone has to work or be absent, they must either call and leave a message or ask a teammate to tell the instructor. If one student doesn't call and is absent, the whole group is deducted one point.

SCANS Competencies

1. Teamwork
2. Teaching Others
3. Leadership
4. Negotiating
5. Allocating time and human resources
6. Understanding systems
7. Responsibility
8. Self-management
9. Integrity/honesty
10. Problem solving

Figure 5.6
New Student Letter

Dear ______________________________________,

This ESL class will give you the opportunity to learn more English and practice using English to communicate at work. Students are organized in teams or groups. In many jobs you will have to work in teams.

You are a member of Team ___________________________ for the next few months. You have a responsibility to yourself and your team to come to the VESL class everyday. If you can't come, please call ____________________________, and leave a message.

This is how points will be given to teams each day:

Attendance: 2 points if all group members are present or if a person is absent but calls or writes a note ***before*** the class.
1 point if a team member is absent without notification.

Participation: 2 points if all group members participate and are respectful during team work time.

Team Jobs: 2 points if the team job is well done.
1 point if the team job is not done well.
1 point if the person who was supposed to do the job didn't do it and another team member had to.
0 points if no member of your team does the job and the teacher has to do it.

Extra Credit: The teacher will tell you when you can get extra points for your team.
Certain homework assignments will be given extra points.

The team work gives you the opportunity to communicate with your classmates. In addition, our classroom will be a nicer, neater, and more organized place to work.

Sincerely,

____

From the classroom of Donna Price-Machado. Reprinted with permission.

Figure 5.7
Trainer Instructions: Team Chart

After the student reads the "New Student Letter," take him or her to the team job chart on the wall. Show the student where the information for his or her team is located on the chart. Help the student find his or her day. Then ask the student the following questions.

1. What is the number of your team?
2. What is the job of your team for this week?
3. What day are you responsible for doing the team job?
4. What are the team points given for?
5. Who are your teammates?
6. What is the purpose of this team chart?

ANSWERS

1. Look at the student's letter or on the wall chart to check the team number.
2. Look at the team job chart if you don't remember the answer.
3. Look at the wall chart if you don't remember the student's day.
4. Attendance and job, participation, some time extra credit assignments.
5. Look at the chart for the names.
6. To communicate more in English, to get to know your classmates, to help the teacher keep the room and materials neater and more organized, to learn to work in teams because you will probably have to do that when you get a job.

From the classroom of Donna Price-Machado. Reprinted with permission.

Teamwork With Lower Level Classes

Team organization for the completion of classroom tasks can also be used effectively with lower level ESL classes. Teachers at the Salinas Adult School have developed a pocket chart with numbered cards representing the different teams, as shown in Figure 5.8. The cards are placed next to the task to which that team has been assigned. Team groupings are posted separately in order to keep the pocket chart as simple as possible. Each week team groupings are changed and the instructor rotates the team cards down the chart to change the team job assignments.

Figure 5.8
Teamwork Assignment Pocket Chart

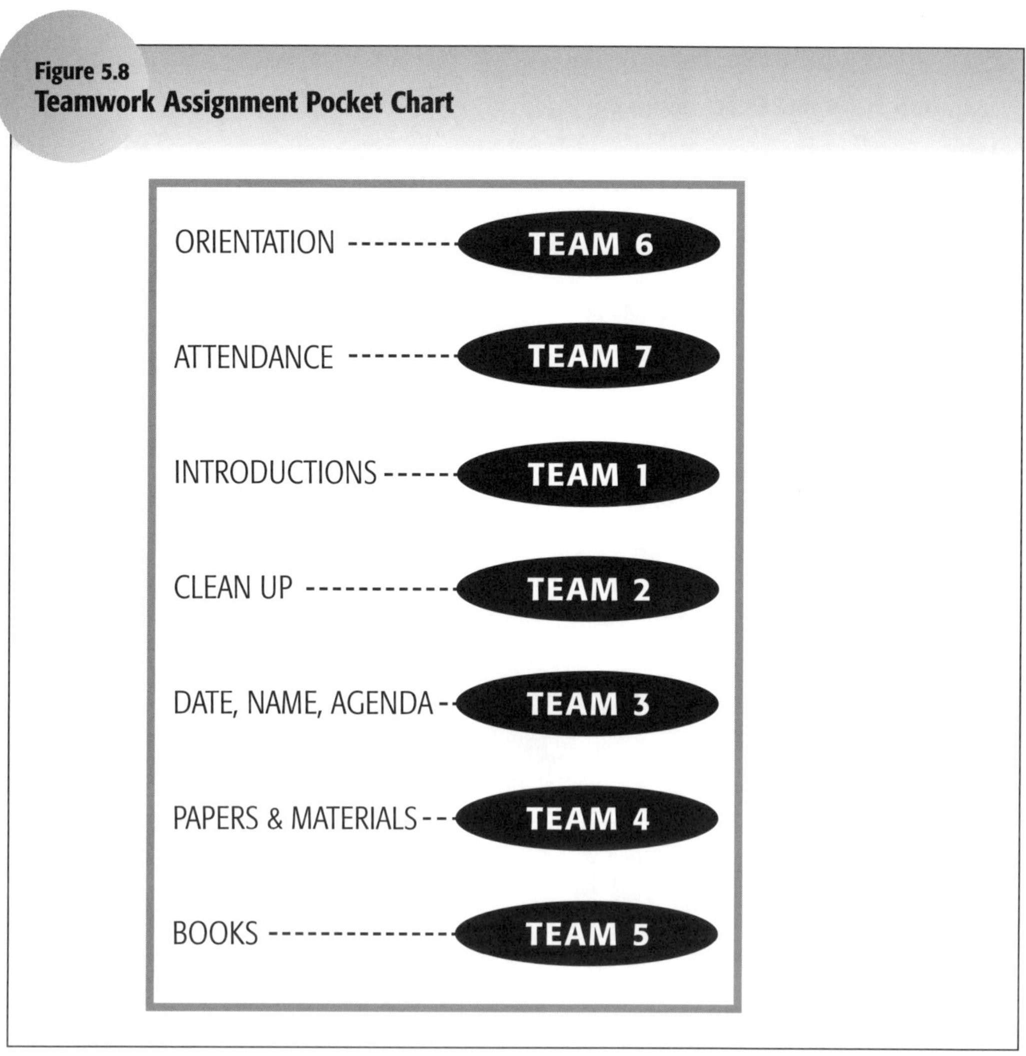

Job Duties Within Teams

Because of fluctuating attendance, it is not always possible to form long-term teams. Many teachers have successfully organized teams on a daily basis by asking team members to take specific roles or jobs for the duration of a single instructional session. Whether teams are formed on a long-term or short-term basis, each class member can be assigned a role or job.

Each role has duties and responsibilities attached to it, with clear performance criteria established in advance. Job descriptions can be posted in the classroom or printed on cards and distributed to team members as jobs are assigned. Instructors can select or adapt the job titles and descriptions in Figure 5.9 to form teams of different sizes.

Figure 5.9
Team Job Titles and Descriptions

Job Title: *Team Leader/Manager*

Description: Organizes assignments, plans necessary activities, selects team members to fulfill each task.

Job Title: *Assistant Team Leader/Manager*

Description: Fills in for leader as needed, provides assistance to team members, trains new team members.

Job Title: *Time Keeper*

Description: Allocates time for each part of an assignment, keeps team members on task, ensures that task is completed within given time frame.

Job Title: *Recorder/Secretary*

Description: Keeps notes and records as necessary; fills out forms, work orders, and group assignment reports.

Job Title: *Evaluator*

Description: Assesses group performance according to specified criteria, makes suggestions for performance improvement.

Job Title: *Grammar Cop*

Description: Monitors oral and written interaction of team members for grammatical errors, suggests improvements and corrections.

Job Title: *Attendance Clerk*

Description: Records attendance of team members, records arrival and departure times as appropriate.

Job Title: *Resource Manager*

Description: Identifies resources needed to complete team assignment, locates, collects, and returns resources as necessary; maintains resources in good condition.

With new teamwork assignments, team members can be given additional responsibility by choosing for themselves the specific jobs they will perform. Instructors can provide guidelines, such as choosing a job that is different from the one held in the previous teamwork assignment, but otherwise, learners can be expected to organize themselves. Additionally, the use of nametags or badges that replicate those worn in the workplace can provide a subtle but powerful reminder of the expectations attached to each role.

Alternatives to Teamwork

Teamwork is not suitable to all groups of learners or in all teaching situations. However, the use of cooperative learning and learner-centered instructional strategies discussed earlier in Section 4 also promote the development of competencies used in the workplace.

Instructors can create a structure that encourages class members to volunteer for individualized tasks for a set period, such as one instructional session or one week. Giving individual learners responsibility for classroom tasks, either voluntarily or by assignment, can provide a foundation on which a more comprehensive system of team assignments can be later based, if appropriate. For refugees and immigrants who have no U.S. work history and few transferable skills, volunteering in the classroom can provide an opportunity to gain valuable work experience and apply the workplace competencies that they are developing. Figure 5.10 lists some possible classroom jobs that can be given as individual assignments.

Figure 5.10
Classroom Job Titles

Job Title: *Resource Allocation Specialist*

Description: Allocates appropriate resources to classmates. Determines type and quantity of resources required. Ensures that all learners receive necessary resources in a timely manner. Troubleshoots equipment. Develops a tracking system and tracks resource distribution and collection. Maintains an inventory of resources. Communicates with classmates and instructor regarding resource needs.

Job Title: *Attendance Secretary*

Description: Counts the initials on the sign-in sheet and the learners in the room. Calls roll if the numbers differ. Makes note of excused and unexcused absences.

Job Title: *File Clerk*

Description: Puts papers into teacher's student files at teacher's request. Files absence excuse papers. Keeps files in alphabetical order.

Job Title: *Librarian*

Description: Collects homework papers for teacher. Counts books, passes them out, collects them, counts again, puts them away.

Job Title: *Custodian*

Description: Turns on lights. Opens blinds. Makes sure trash is collected and thrown away.

Classroom Management Techniques and the National Reporting System

The broad skill levels outlined by the NRS (Figure 1.3) require instructors in state-administered federally funded programs to evaluate learners' abilities in relation to basic life skills. By using the classroom management techniques described in this section, instructors are giving learners opportunities to develop and practice these skills. Both teamwork and individual assignments offer opportunities for expressing needs; interpreting signs, charts, and other graphics; and following, giving, and clarifying oral and written instructions. Thus, learners are actively engaged in developing and using English effectively in both work and social situations as identified by the NRS, the EFF, and the SCANS. The importance of active engagement in the learning process is addressed further in Section 6.

SECTION SIX

Developing Active Learning Through Reflection, Skills Transfer, and Authentic Assessment

Underlying both EFF and SCANS is an emphasis on the importance of active learning, that is, engagement in one's own learning process for success in the workplace and the wider community. Lifelong learning skills include taking responsibility for learning, reflecting and evaluating, learning through research, and using information and communication technology. To become active learners, adults need to know why they are learning the content and processes they are and where and how they will use them. In short, learners need to

- have the skills that they and other stakeholders are seeking,
- know that they have them, and
- show that they have them.

Learners need opportunities to reflect on learning, to demonstrate their ability to apply what they have learned, and to evaluate their own progress. Reflection and demonstration are especially important because there is no quick and easy way to demonstrate mastery of every competency on multiple-choice and other pencil-and-paper tests. Learners who have been given the opportunity to develop and practice language and life skills through carefully crafted activities are more likely to be able to transfer learned information from one context to another. Their self-confidence will probably also increase. Therefore, reflection, demonstration, and evaluation activities are authentic ways to assess learner progress and can have significant impact on pencil-and-paper-test performance.

Encouraging Active Learning Through Reflection

To become independent, active learners, students need time in each instructional session to reflect on what they have done, how they have done it, and how they feel about it. In a workplace-oriented classroom, this reflection must encompass both the content material covered and the workplace competencies that have been practiced.

The content in an ESL class consists of the basic language students are learning (vocabulary, phrases, grammar); how they use it (functions and competencies); and what it sounds like (pronunciation, intonation). Reflection activities can and should be designed to address all of these areas. They may take the form of individual reflection followed by guided whole-group discussion or peer review. Below are examples of tools and activities that promote reflection.

Agenda Review

Using a daily agenda provides a structure for focused reflection throughout an instructional session. The agenda mirrors the instructor's lesson plan and shows the stages of the instructional session, including the time assigned toward the end of the session for reflection. The instructor can check off each agenda item as it is covered or ask a learner or team to take responsibility for doing this (Figure 6.1).

Figure 6.1
Daily Agenda

AGENDA – May 14, 2002

1. Greetings – special occasions? ✔
2. Review – short and long answers ✔
3. Review – contractions and pronouns ✔
4. Short-term and long-term goals ✔
5. Note taking and active listening skills ✔
6. Team activity ✔
7. Goals chart ✔
8. Reflection – what did we do?
9. Homework assignment

Textbook Contents Page Check-Off

For instructors who use an assigned classroom textbook, a simple way of giving learners the opportunity to reflect on the content they have covered is to ask them to check off sections from the contents page as they finish each section. This strategy allows learners to see that the language and content material is being presented in an organized and systematic way. Some textbooks have their contents pages set up as checklists. Others include checklists in their assessment activities at the end of each chapter, as in Figure 6.2.

Figure 6.2
End-of-Chapter Assessment Checklist

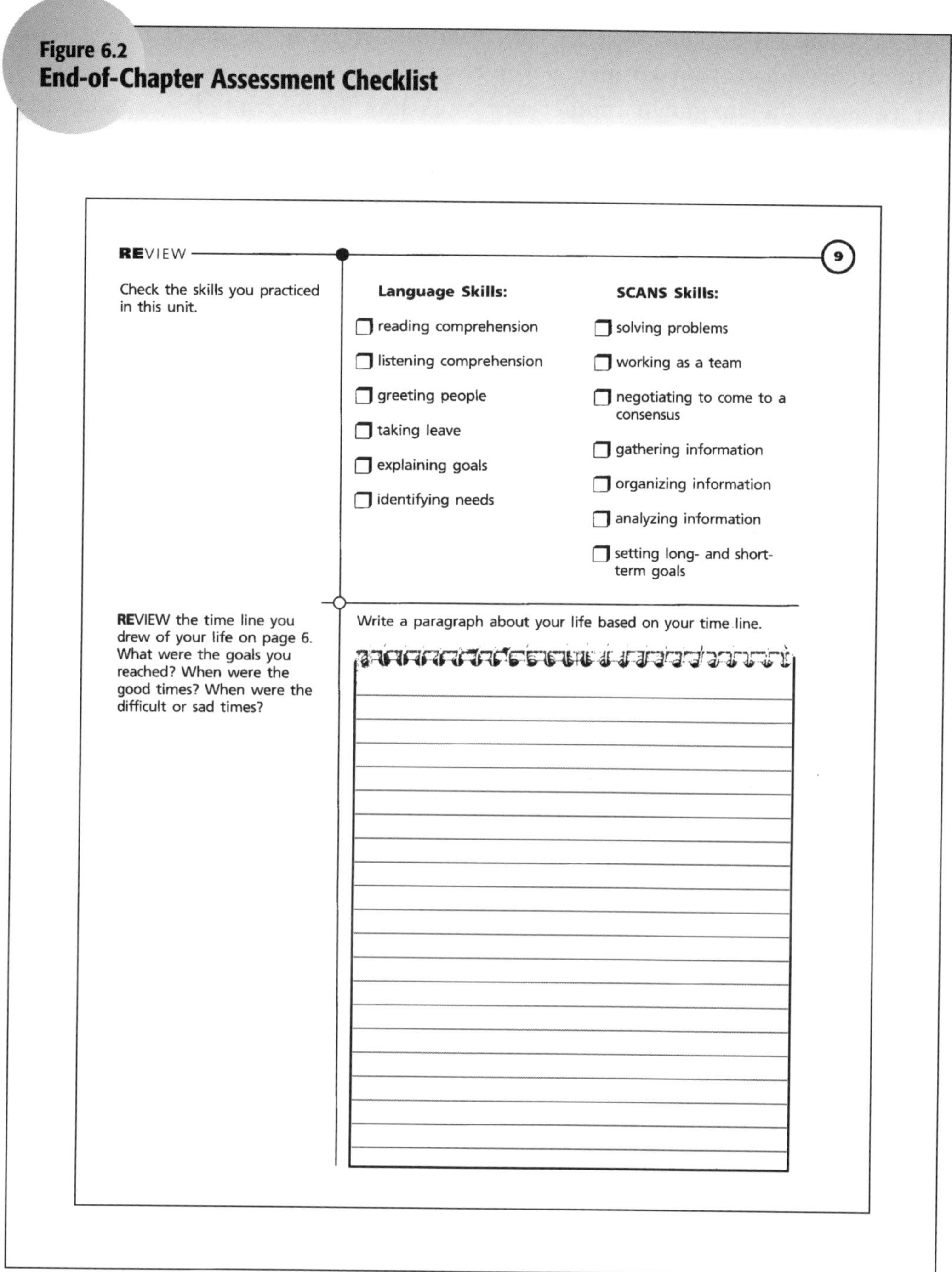

REVIEW

9

Check the skills you practiced in this unit.

Language Skills:

- ❐ reading comprehension
- ❐ listening comprehension
- ❐ greeting people
- ❐ taking leave
- ❐ explaining goals
- ❐ identifying needs

SCANS Skills:

- ❐ solving problems
- ❐ working as a team
- ❐ negotiating to come to a consensus
- ❐ gathering information
- ❐ organizing information
- ❐ analyzing information
- ❐ setting long- and short-term goals

REVIEW the time line you drew of your life on page 6. What were the goals you reached? When were the good times? When were the difficult or sad times?

Write a paragraph about your life based on your time line.

From *A Day in the Life of the González Family* (p. 9), by C. Van Duzer & M. Burt, 1999, Washington, DC, and McHenry, IL: Center for Applied Linguistics & Delta Systems. Reprinted with permission.

For beginning-level classes, this reflection activity can be done as a group. With an overhead transparency or flip chart of the contents page, the instructor reviews the language competency that has been covered, checking the appropriate item on the contents page and directing learners to do the same on their copies. Because the grammar points listed on the contents page may not be meaningful to some learners, it may be better to direct them to reflect on what they have learned in terms of language competencies. For example, it

Figure 6.3
Table of Contents Assessment Checklist

Contents

	COMPETENCIES	GRAMMAR
To the Teacher Page viii		
Step-by-Step Teaching Procedures Page x		
UNIT 1 Introductions Page 1	Introduce yourself and others. Ask for, give, spell, and write your first and last name. Ask where someone is from and say where you are from. Identify things in a classroom and follow classroom instructions.	present tense of *be* *What?, Where?* *my, your, his, her* imperatives
UNIT 2 Family and Friends Page 13	Greet someone. Ask about the names and relationships of the people in someone's family. Give the names and relationships of the people in your family. Ask someone to repeat for clarification and repeat when someone asks you to. Ask for someone's area code and phone number. Give and write your own area code and phone number.	present tense of *be:* *yes/no* questions, *yes/no* short answers *Who?* *this, that, these, those, their*
UNIT 3 School Page 25	Ask and say where things are in your classroom and where places are in your school. Give your teacher's name, your class level, and your room number. Repeat something to check your understanding. Give and write your first language and your age.	present tense of *be* *Where?, How old?* noun plurals *its, our* *on, next to* (location)
UNIT 4 Community Services Page 37	Report an emergency and give the location. Ask and say where places are in your community. Ask for someone's address. Give and write your own address.	present tense of *be* *there is/there are* *a, an* *between, on the corner of, in, on, at* (location)
UNIT 5 Shopping Page 49	Ask where things are in a store and read aisle numbers. Ask for and read prices and the total amount. Identify bills and coins.	present continuous tense pro-predicate *do (What are you doing?)* *How much is? How much are?*

is more meaningful for learners to know that they can introduce themselves and ask someone else where they are from, but it is less meaningful to say they can use the present tense of the verb "to be."

The table of contents from *Crossroads 1* lists both competencies and the grammar term for each competency (Figure 6.3).

	COMPETENCIES	GRAMMAR
UNIT 6 **Housing** Page 61	On the phone: answer, give your name, ask for someone, say that someone is not there. Ask "Who is it?" when someone is at the door; identify yourself at someone's door. Report problems in the house. Name the rooms and furniture in a house.	present continuous tense: negative statements, *yes / no* questions, *yes / no* short answers
UNIT 7 **Recreation** Page 73	Invite someone to do something, respond to an invitation, and agree on a day. Ask about someone's weekly activities and state your own. Ask and tell someone the time. Write your Social Security number.	simple present tense: *yes / no* questions, *yes / no* short answers
UNIT 8 **Health** Page 85	Report health problems, name parts of your body, and follow instructions in a medical examination. Say and respond to "Thank you" and "Goodbye." State your marital status and show it on a form. Write your name with your middle initial.	simple present tense: negative statements *feel* + adjective
UNIT 9 **Transportation** Page 97	Say where you are going, ask where the bus goes, and ask where to get off. Read bus destination and street signs. Ask for, give, and follow directions. Give the streets and a landmark near your house.	simple present tense imperatives *Where?, When?, How?*
UNIT 10 **Employment** Page 109	Read and respond to warning signs. Ask to use someone's things and respond to such a request. Name some jobs and state your own job. Give and write dates and sign your name.	simple present tense negative imperatives
Grammar Summaries Page 121		
Tapescript For Listening Plus Page 124		
Basic Conversations For Progress Checks Page 129		

From *Crossroads 1* (pp. vi-vii), by I. Frankel & C. Meyers, 1991, New York: Oxford University Press. Reprinted with permission.

Literacy-level texts for adult English language learners often incorporate pictures into the book, which can be used to preview and review topics. Figure 6.4 shows two pages from a textbook that does this by including pictures in the table of contents and by displaying pictures on the first page of each chapter.

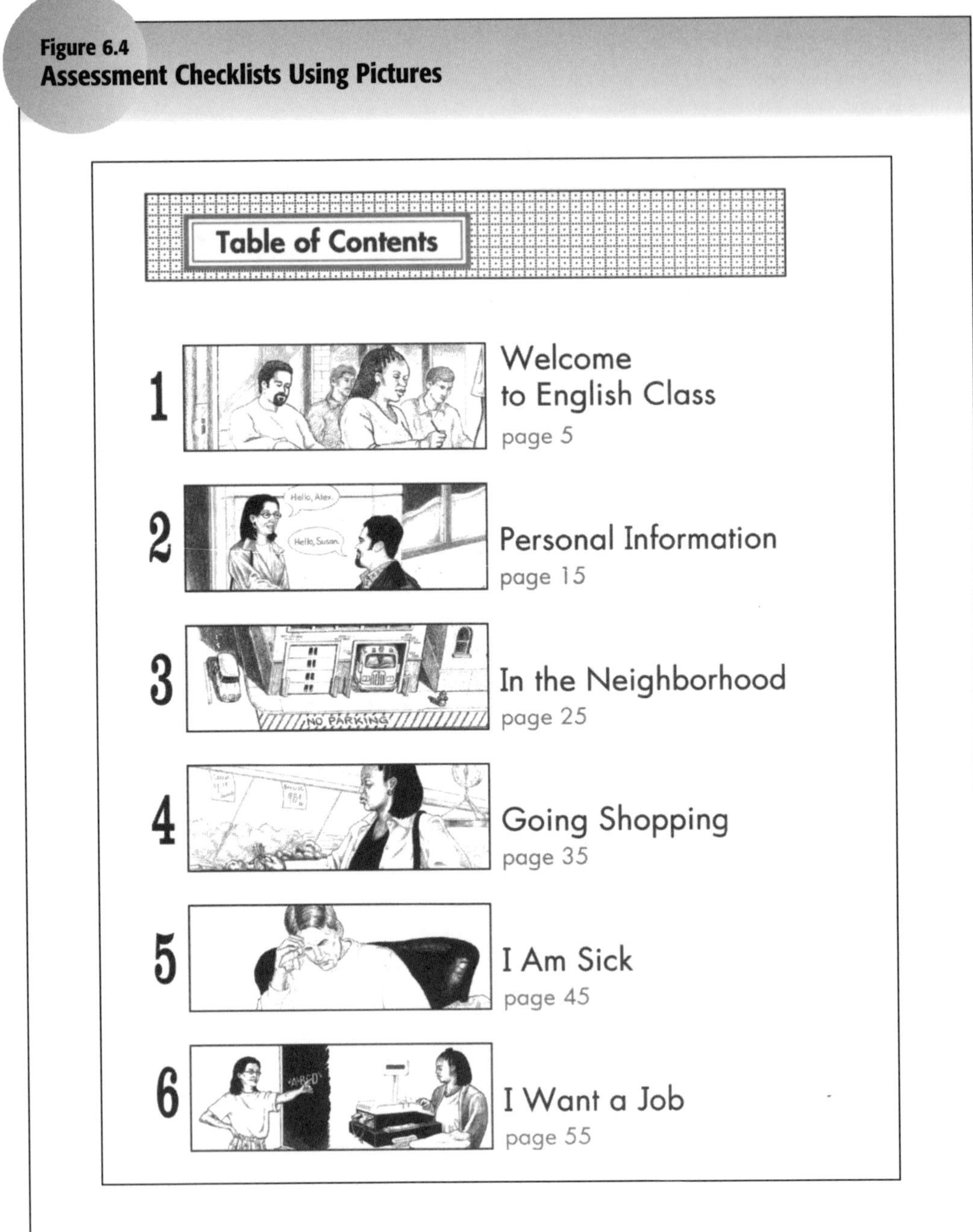

Figure 6.4
Assessment Checklists Using Pictures

Table of Contents

From *LifePrints Literacy: ESL for Adults* (pp. 3, 55), by M. C. Florez, 2002, Syracuse, NY: New Readers Press.
Reprinted with permission.

Language-Learning Diaries

Language-learning diaries can be used as a reflection activity with learners at all levels. Learners can write in their diaries on a daily or weekly basis. Beginning-level learners can complete a list of statements (Worksheet 6.1).

Progress Graphs

Although instructors may see their learners making strides in learning the language, learners themselves often do not share this perspective unless they are guided through activities that document their progress. Each learner can maintain a simple progress graph for activities that take place on a regular basis. Figure 6.5 shows two graphs used to track learners' achievements on weekly spelling tests and dictations. Scores for the spelling tests are shown on a bar graph; scores for the dictations are shown on a line graph. When directing learners to observe the pattern of their scores, instructors can ask questions about the correlation between attendance, studying for the test, and the number of correct responses.

WORKSHEET 6.1

Beginning-Level Diary

Complete the following statements:

Today I learned ______________________________.

Today I read ______________________________ in English.

Today I spoke English to ______________________________.

Today I wanted to speak when ______________________________.

Today I learned some new words. They are ______________________________

______________________________.

Tomorrow I am going to ______________________________.

Figure 6.5
Progress Graphs

Spelling Test Progress Graph

Number Correct												
10				■								
9	■			■		■						
8	■		■	■		■						
7	■	■	■	■	■	■						
6	■	■	■	■	■	■						
5	■	■	■	■	■	■						
4	■	■	■	■	■	■						
3	■	■	■	■	■	■						
2	■	■	■	■	■	■						
1	■	■	■	■	■	■						
Test No.	1	2	3	4	5	6	7	8	9	10	11	12

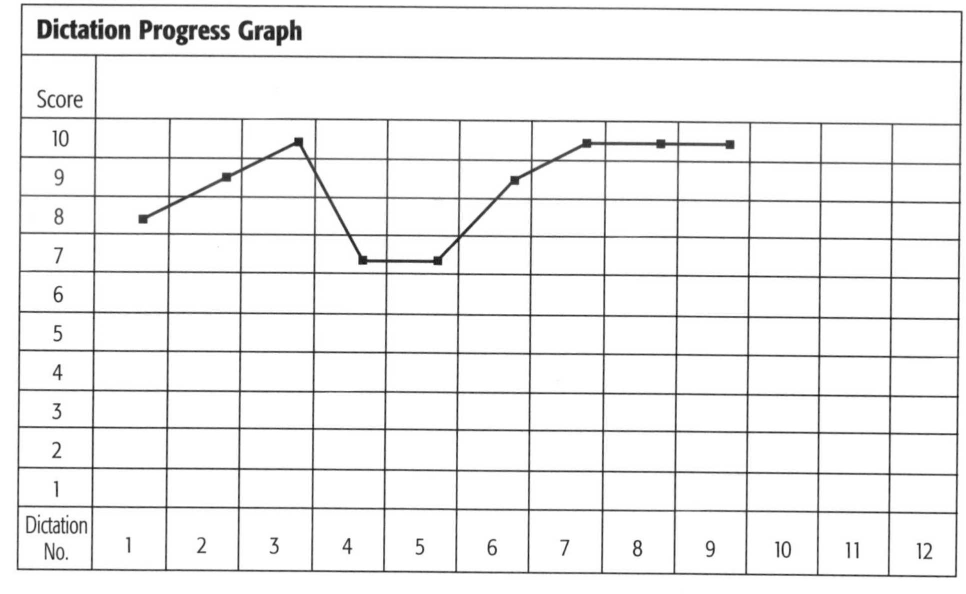

Developed by Donna Price-Machado. Reprinted with permission.

Peer Review Activities

Given large class sizes and limited hours of class instruction, it is often difficult for instructors to devote a great deal of time to individual learners. Involving learners in guided peer-review activities provides opportunities for them to reflect on how the language they are producing sounds to others (Worksheet 6.2). In high-level classes, peer-review activities are effective for generating reflective thinking about writing assignments (Worksheet 6.3).

Peer review need not be limited to advanced-level learners. Learners at all levels can be expected, before they turn in assignments, to have a classmate review their homework, projects, and other written work. To document this peer review, reviewers can place their initials in the top corner of the page or attach a short response form (Worksheet 6.4).

WORKSHEET 6.2

Focused-Listening Peer Review

Who is reading? ______________________ Who is listening? ____________________

Circle the answer while your partner is reading.

1. Did your partner's voice go down at the end of each sentence?
   always often rarely never
2. Did your partner read very fast?
   always often rarely never
3. Were there any words that you didn't understand when your partner said them?
   Tell him/her what those words were in a polite way.
   Here are some polite ways to help someone:
   Could you repeat that word, please?
   I think you should say ____
   If I were you, I would say it like this: ________________________________
4. Did your partner say some words quieter than other words?
   always often rarely never
5. Did your partner say the stressed syllables louder than the unstressed syllables?
   always often rarely never

From the classroom of Donna Price-Machado. Reprinted with permission.

WORKSHEET 6.3

Peer Response Form

Do the following peer response after you read the short article and write your own summary.

Writer's name: ____________________

Peer's (checker's) name: ____________________

Peer Response

1. Does the writer give the source at the beginning? Yes/No
2. Does the writer give the main idea in his/her own words? Yes/No
3. Does the writer use the present tense? Yes/No
4. Does the writer give some supporting evidence? Yes/No
5. Do you think the writer really understood the article? Yes/No
   If you said "no," ask the writer to explain orally.

WORKSHEET 6.4

Beginning-Level Peer Review Form

Date: ____________________

Reviewer's Name: ____________________

I am reviewing ____________________'s work.

I checked

- [ ] Grammar
- [ ] Punctuation
- [ ] Spelling

The peer-review process can also promote class discussion about the function of peer review in the workplace. In the workplace as in the class, written reports are often submitted by teams rather than by individuals. One employee usually writes the report, and co-workers review it, giving suggestions to improve content and style before the report is sent to the supervisor.

Reflecting on Affective Experiences in the Classroom

Learners need opportunities to reflect on learning. During reflection activities, instructors can ask learners to identify activities that they liked, disliked, or found too easy, too complicated, or too difficult.

Some learning activities may generate a high level of anxiety. For example, making oral presentations to the class requires learners to produce language under stressful conditions. Having the opportunity to reflect on the experience allows each learner greater understanding and ownership of the learning process (see Worksheet 6.5).

WORKSHEET 6.5

Reflection on Oral Presentations

Name ______________________________ Date ______________

1. What did you like about doing the presentation?
2. What didn't you like about doing the presentation?
3. Are you pleased with your performance?
   Explain what you are proud of.
4. What would you like to improve about your performance?
5. Are you pleased with your team's performance?
   Explain what you liked and didn't like about what they did.
6. If we do this activity again, how would you change it?

Some reflection activities can be adapted for use with beginning-level learners. Worksheet 6.6 shows a mood-indicator chart using pictures and words, which allows learners to reflect on and describe their feelings about what is happening in class.

Active Learning Through Awareness of How Skills Transfer

Learners need to identify ways that they can apply what they are learning in class to what they do in their jobs and in their everyday lives. Instructors can help learners recognize how they can use these skills in other areas of their lives. For example, when conducting an oral review of the workplace competencies that learners have practiced, instructors can ask them to give examples of other situations in which they could use each competency, asking questions such as, "Did you do problem-solving today? What did you do? Do you solve problems at work? Do you solve problems at home or at your child's school? Give me an example."

Focused Journal or Logbook Entries

Perhaps the most direct way to give learners an understanding of the relevance of what they do in class to what they do in life is to ask them to write focused journal or logbook entries. This activity has been used for many years in both K-12 and adult education classes (Peyton, 2000).

WORKSHEET 6.6

Mood-Indicator Chart

Name ______________________________

Circle one answer:

1. Today, I feel... a) good b) bad c) OK ...about the class.

2. Today the class was... a) easy b) bad c) OK

3. I feel... a) happy b) unhappy c) O.K. ...about working in teams.

At least twice a week, Price-Machado asks her learners to write logbook entries that specifically relate something that has happened in class to their roles in the community, in their children's schools, or at work. The following entry by one of her learners indicates the connections that learners can make through this activity:

> Today in the class you said something important for me because I do it yesterday in my work. You'll said is a good idea take notes when somebody explain something to you. And that's what I did yesterday when my boss explained to me how to use the cash register. I telled her when I don't understand or I'm confused to explain me again and I repeat to her what I understand to know if its right or wrong. I asked her if sometimes can I see my notes to check if I'm doing it right. Her answer was yes because the notes can help you a lot in you work. (D. Price-Machado, personal communication, 2000)

Because the purpose of this activity is to provide an opportunity for reflection on application of skills learned in the classroom, the instructor does not correct grammar and spelling errors in learners' journals.

Checklists

Learners can use checklists to document completion of activities that demonstrate specific competencies. In order to check off the successful demonstration of a competency, a learner must be able to

- describe the completed classroom activity that demonstrated ability in the competency,
- give an example of a situation in which the competency is applied in the workplace, and
- give an example of a situation in which the competency is applied in another area of the learner's life.

Figure 6.6 is an example of an individual learner's SCANS Resources Competency Checklist.

Figure 6.6
SCANS Resources Competency Checklist

Resources Competency Students demonstrate that they can…		**Dates Demonstrated**	**Classroom Activity**	**Workplace Situation**	**Other Situation**
1. Prepare and follow schedules	✔	11/15/01 - 11/30/01	Team made and followed a 2–week schedule to complete the end of unit of project	Shift and vacation schedules	Parent volunteers snack schedule at at daughter's pre-school
2. Organize and distribute resources	✔				
3. Keep records	✔	11/01/01 - 11/30/01	I tracked my attendance and spelling test and dictation scores	Inventory lists Time sheets	Photo log of Cambodian community dance troupe performances
4. Evaluate performance and give feedback					

Active Learning Through Assessment of Competencies

Classroom assessment can be defined as an approach to collecting focused feedback, early and often, on learners' current knowledge, skills, and instructional preferences, and on how well they are learning what we are teaching (Kinsella, 1997). Assessment provides teachers and learners with information and insights needed to improve teaching effectiveness and learner acquisition of knowledge and skills. Instructors need to document individual learners' mastery of competencies, but learners themselves should be actively involved in the evaluation of how they are doing, what they have learned, how well they can use the new skills, and where and when they will use them.

Since many competencies do not lend themselves to assessment by pencil-and-paper tests, the instructor must identify ways in which learners can demonstrate their ability of these skills. Reflection and skills-transfer activities provide a mechanism for this. Key to authentic assessment, however, is identifying the behaviors that characterize each competency.

To identify behaviors that demonstrate a learner's ability in a specific workplace or civics competency, instructors can ask themselves, "What does someone who is competent in this area actually do? What is the observable and measurable action that will demonstrate this skill?" For example, a worker who demonstrates competency in the EFF "Planning" Standard can define a goal in realistic terms, identify and carry out an achievable series of action steps, develop a system to document progress toward the goal, and develop a way of evaluating the plan's effectiveness. To determine a student's competence at planning, instructors can evaluate the extent to which a learner is able to do the five skills listed in Worksheet 6.7.

Monitoring Progress

Learners can use personal checklists to document that they have demonstrated specific competencies. Checklists can be used by learners at all levels of instruction. Although learners rate themselves qualitatively, and their assessments will therefore be subjective, this is a useful activity because it can help instill in learners a sense or responsibility for their own learning.

WORKSHEET 6.7

Planning Evaluation

On (date) ____________________,

Student was able to	***Achievement Scale***
	1 (Somewhat) 2 (Satisfactory) 3 (Well)
1. Identify and describe goal	_____
2. Create action steps	_____
3. Follow action steps	_____
4. Track progress	_____
5. Judge success	_____
Cumulative Score =	_____ (out of possible 15)

By asking learners to set attendance, preparedness, and activity goals for themselves each week, the instructor can translate the EFF "Planning" Standard to classroom application. Learners record their goals and monitor their progress. Personal goal setting and progress monitoring become both observable and measurable (see Worksheets 6.8 and 6.9).

WORKSHEET 6.8

Class Time Card

Student Name________________________________ Phone #___________________________

Room # ___________________________ Supervisor _________________________________

Week ________________ Attendance goal for week of _____________ = ________ hours

Day	Date	Time In	Time Out	Total Time
Monday				
Tuesday				
Wednesday				
Thursday				
Friday				

Total number of hours of attendance for week of _____________ = ________ hours

☐ I met my attendance goal this week.

☐ I did not meet my attendance goal this week.

☐ I missed my attendance goal this week by __________ hours.

Adapted with permission from Sue Pratt, Fremont Adult School.

Active Learner Progress Charts

A chart on which learners assign themselves scores each day (Worksheet 6.10) can be used to assess their progress toward becoming actively involved in their own learning. These progress charts also provide excellent material for learner-teacher discussions on areas that need development or in which a learner is lacking self-confidence.

Team Evaluation Charts

When learners work in teams, they should be given the opportunity to reflect on their team's performance and their own performance as team members. Team evaluation charts can be used for this (Worksheet 6.11). One team member, acting as the team evaluator, can evaluate the entire group, or all the team members can fill out the form together.

WORKSHEET 6.9

Progress Chart

THIS WEEK			➡ AGREE ➡			
I made an effort to reach my goals.	1	2	3	4	5	6
I worked well with my team.	1	2	3	4	5	6
I did my homework.	1	2	3	4	5	6
I solved problems.	1	2	3	4	5	6
I stopped working when asked to.	1	2	3	4	5	6
I used every minute of my time.	1	2	3	4	5	6
I felt good about myself.	1	2	3	4	5	6
I did not copy from others.	1	2	3	4	5	6
I made decisions.	1	2	3	4	5	6
I helped others.	1	2	3	4	5	6

WORKSHEET 6.10

Active Learner Progress Chart

Class: ______________________ Week of: ______________

Name: ______________________________________

Active Learner Classroom Behaviors	**Mon**	**Tues**	**Wed**	**Thurs**	**Fri**	**Total**
I arrived to class on time.						
I brought materials/ equipment (pen, paper, handouts, etc.).						
I brought the textbook.						
I completed all homework before class.						
I made eye contact with the teacher.						
I made eye contact with my team members.						
I answered a question voluntarily.						
I participated well in my team.						
I made notes.						
I wrote down the homework assignment.						
I told the teacher when I did not understand.						
I learned new things.						
I did my best.						

Adapted with permission from Kate Kinsella, CATESOL Conference, (1997). Fresno, California.

WORKSHEET 6.11

Team Evaluation Charts

Team Evaluation

Work Team: ______________________________

On a scale of 1-5 (5 is high), rate the performance of your team:

Overall performance ________

Ability to work cooperatively ________

Ability to get the job done ________

Ability to do the job on time ________

Ability to use resources efficiently ________

Who is team member of the day? Why?

____

____

What problems did your team have?

____

____

What recommendations do you have to improve team performance?

____

____

Team Evaluation

Work Team: ______________________________

Did everyone come on time? Yes No

How many people were late? _______

Did everyone bring paper, pens, pencils, and books/binders? Yes No

How many people forgot things? _______

Circle a number: (5 is the best score).

Did your team do a good job?	5	4	3	2	1
Did you help each other?	5	4	3	2	1
Did you finish on time?	5	4	3	2	1

Who did a very good job? ______________________________

What did they do? ______________________________

Evaluator's name: ______________________________

Assessment in Relation to the NRS

In programs that are required to report learner progress in compliance with the National Reporting System for Adult Education (NRS), instructors must administer and score performance-based assessments in accordance with procedures and rubrics mandated by the state. Instructors can, at the same time, help learners evaluate their own progress in relation to the standards, especially for the functional and workplace skills identified in the level descriptors (Figure 1.3). One effective way to do this is to make explicit connections between in-class activities and the functional and workplace skills. A simple questionnaire (Worksheet 6.12) can point out these connections while encouraging learners to reflect on their own skill development.

Instructors need to know that they are teaching the language and skills required by their learners in the workplace and the community and that learners are making progress in their acquisition of language and basic skills. At the same time, learners need to know how and why they are learning what they are learning; they need to be able to see and reflect on the progress they are making; and they need to learn strategies, such as those described in this section, to transfer the language and skills learned in the classroom to the world outside the classroom where they live and work.

WORKSHEET 6.12

NRS Functional and Workplace Skills Questionaire		
SKILL	***When do you use this skill in class?***	***How is your ability to use this skill different or better now than before you started this class?***
Read signs		
Read maps and diagrams		
Read and follow instructions		
Fill out forms		
Take phone messages		
Make graphs, charts, and diagrams		
Write reports		
Use computers and other equipment		

A FINAL NOTE

In a successful program, content is carefully selected to reflect the priorities identified by students and external stakeholders. The language skills that learners and other stakeholders consider important are also emphasized. Instructional activities are learner centered, engaging participants in active learning and requiring them to accept responsibility for the learning that takes place in the classroom. Instructional activities and classroom management techniques provide opportunities for learners to develop workplace and civic competencies and to apply what they are learning to the reality of their everyday lives. A successful program produces outcomes that are responsive to the goals of all stakeholders, and in so doing, prepares students to be successful in the workplace and in the wider community.

ESL programs are challenged to navigate among the demands of all the stakeholders who seek to define the parameters of what will be taught and how it will be taught. In order to produce outcomes that are recognized as successful by all critical stakeholders, instructors need to prepare adult English language learners for participation in the workplace and wider community. Program staff must concentrate their energies on finding a way to reconcile the agendas of these stakeholders in ways that render them mutually supportive. Such integration is required to protect the integrity of high quality, learner-centered ESL instruction and to ensure the future of adult ESL programs.

LIST OF FIGURES AND WORKSHEETS

Figures

Worksheets

REFERENCES

Adkins, M. A., & Berman, D. (1999). *Mental health and the adult refugee: The role of the ESL teacher.* ERIC Digest. Washington, DC: National Center for ESL Literacy Education. (ERIC Document Reproduction Service No. ED439625) Available: http://www.cal.org/ncle/digests/mental.htm

American Management Association. (2001). *2001 AMA survey on workplace testing: Basic skills, job skills, and psychological measurement.* New York: Author. Available: http://www.amanet.org/research/pdfs/bjp_2001.pdf

Arlington Education and Employment Program. (1994). *The REEP curriculum: A learner-centered ESL curriculum for adults.* (3rd ed.). Arlington, VA: Arlington County Public Schools. (ERIC Document Reproduction Service No. ED397695)

Barton, P., & Jenkins, L. (1995). *Literacy and dependency: The literacy skills of welfare recipients in the United States.* Princeton, NJ: Educational Testing Service.

Bell, J. (1988). *Teaching multilevel classes in ESL.* San Diego, CA: Dormac.

Bransford, J. D., Brown, A. L., & Cockings, R. R. (Eds.). (1999). *How people learn: Brain, mind, experience, and school.* Washington, DC: National Academy Press. (ERIC Document Reproduction Service No. ED440122)

Burt, M., & Keenan, F. (1995). *Adult ESL Learner Assessment: Purposes and Tools. ERIC Digest.* Washington, DC: National Center for ESL Literacy Education. (ERIC Document Reproduction Service No. ED386962) Available: http://www.cal.org/ncle/digests/KEENAN.HTM

Carnevale, A., & Desrochers, D. (1999). *Getting down to business: Matching welfare recipients' skills to jobs that train.* Princeton, NJ: Educational Testing Service.

Comings, J. P., Parrella A., & Soricone, L. (1999, December). *Persistence among adult basic education students in pre-GED classes.* (NCSALL Report #12). Cambridge, MA: National Center for the Study of Adult Learning and Literacy, Harvard Graduate School of Education. Available: http://gseweb.harvard.edu/~ncsall/research/reports.htm

Council of Economic Advisors. (1998). *Good news for low income families: Expansion in the earned income tax credit and the minimum wage.* Washington, DC: Author. http://clinton3.nara.gov/WH/EOP/CEA/html/eitc.pdf

D'Amico, D. (1997). *Adult education and welfare-to-work initiatives: A review of research, practice, and policy.* Washington, DC: National Institute for Literacy.

Fellows, M. (1998). *Connections: Learners as producers.* Fallbrook, CA: Bright Ideas.

Grognet, A. G. (1996). *Planning, implementing, and evaluating workplace ESL programs.* ERIC Digest. Washington, DC: National Center for ESL Literacy Education. (ERIC Document Reproduction Service No. ED406866) Available: http://www.cal.org/ncle/digests/PLANNINGQA.HTM

Kinsella, K. (1997, April). *Classroom assessment techniques: Tools for improving teaching and learning.* Paper presented at the annual conference of California Teachers of English to Speakers of Other Languages (CATESOL), Fresno, CA.

Knowles, M. S. (1984). The art and science of helping adults learn. In M. S. Knowles et al. (Eds.), *Andragogy in action: Applying modern principles of adult learning.* San Francisco: Jossey Bass.

Moss, D., & Van Duzer, C. (1998). *Project-based learning for adult English language learners.* ERIC Digest. Washington, DC: National Center for ESL Literacy Education. (ERIC Document Reproduction Service No. ED427556) Available: http://www.cal.org/ncle/digests/ProjBase.htm

National Education Goals Panel. (1993). 1993 *National Education Goals report: Building a nation of learners.* Washington, DC: Author. http://www.negp.gov/page1-5.htm

National Institute for Literacy. (n.d.). *Workforce literacy.* Fact sheet. Washington, DC: Author. Available: http://www.nifl.gov/newworld/WORKFORC.HTM

National Reporting System for Adult Education (NRS). (2001, March). *Measures and methods for the National Reporting System for Adult Education: Implementation guidelines.* Washington, DC: U.S. Department of Education, Office of Vocational and Adult Education, Division of Adult Education and Literacy. Available: http://www.air-dc.org/nrs/implement.pdf

Personal Responsibility and Work Opportunity Reconciliation Act of 1996. Pub. L. No. 104-193, 110 Stat. 2105 (1996). Available: http://www.nifl.gov/lincs/collections/policy/welfare.html

Peyton, J. K. (2000). *Dialogue journals: Interactive writing to develop language and literacy.* ERIC Q&A. Washington, DC: National Center for ESL Literacy Education. (ERIC Document Reproduction Service No. ED450614) Available: http://www.cal.org/ncle/digests/Dialogue_Journals.HTML

Price-Machado, D. (1996, December). *Workplace attitudes: A lesson.* CATESOL News, p. 4.

Secretary's Commission on Achieving Necessary Skills (SCANS). (1991). *What work requires of schools: A SCANS report for America 2000.* Washington, DC: U.S. Department of Labor.

Secretary's Commission on Achieving Necessary Skills (SCANS). (1993). *Teaching the SCANS competencies.* Washington, DC: U.S. Department of Labor. Available: http://wdr.doleta.gov/opr/FULLTEXT/93-teaching_scans.pdf

Stein, S. (2000). *Equipped for the future content standards: What adults need to know and be able to do in the 21st century.* Washington, DC: National Institute for Literacy.

Sticht, T. G. (1999). *Open entry/open exit: Can teachers teach and adult students learn under this policy for adult education?* El Cajon, CA: Applied Behavior and Cognitive Sciences.

Vella, J. (1994). *Learning to listen, learning to teach: The power of dialogue in educating adults.* San Francisco: Jossey Bass.

Weddel, K. S., & Van Duzer, C. (1997). *Needs assessment for adult ESL learners.* ERIC Digest. Washington DC: National Center for ESL Literacy Education. (ERIC Document Reproduction Service No. ED407882) Available: http://www.cal.org/ncle/digests/Needas.htm

Wislofsky, C. (n.d.). *Jigsaw reading activities.* San Diego, CA: San Diego Community College. (Available from C. Wislofsky, ESL Department, West City Center, 3249 Fordham Street, San Diego, CA 92110; cwislofs@sdccd.net)

Workforce Investment Act of 1998, Pub. L. No. 105-220, § 212, Stat. 936 (1998). Available: http://www.usworkforce.org/asp/act.asp

Wrigley, H. S. (1992). *Learner assessment in adult ESL literacy.* ERIC Q&A. Washington, DC: National Clearinghouse for ESL Literacy Education. (ERIC Document Reproduction Service No. ED353863) Available: http://www.cal.org/ncle/digests/AssessQA.htm.

ADDITIONAL RESOURCES

Arlington Education and Employment Program (REEP). (1997). *Project based learning and assessment: A resource manual for teachers.* Arlington, VA: Arlington Public Schools. (ERIC Document Reproduction Service No. ED442306)

This resource kit explains the purpose and use of project work as a practical and meaningful way of learning English and assessing progress, and it guides teachers in developing projects for learning and assessment.

Basic English Skills Test (BEST)
Center for Applied Linguistics
4646 40th Street NW
Washington, DC 20016-1859
202-362-0700
http://www.cal.org/BEST/

The BEST, developed by adult ESL practitioners with the assistance of language-testing professionals at the Center for Applied Linguistics, is a measurement tool designed for adult ESL learners at the survival and pre-employment skills levels. The test has two sections: oral interview and literacy skills. It provides student performance levels (SPLs) that correlate to the National Reporting Standards (NRS) of the U.S. Department of Education, Office of Vocational and Adult Education (OVAE).

Belfiore, M. E., & Burnaby, B. (Eds.). (1995). *Teaching English in the Workplace.* (2nd ed.). Toronto, Ontario, Canada: Pippin & OISE Press.

This revised and expanded edition of the 1984 publication was written primarily for ESL teachers, but it is a useful tool for anyone involved in workplace ESL, including managers, union representatives, workplace program coordinators, and ESL administrators. A compilation from many experts in the field, the book outlines practices and principles that can apply to a variety of learners in a variety of workplace settings.

CASAS Life Skills Tests
CASAS
5151 Murphy Canyon Road, Suite 220
San Diego, CA 92123-4339
858-292-2900 or 800-255-1036
http://www.casas.org/

CASAS provides tools and resources for adult assessment, instruction, and evaluation. The ESL Appraisal provides an initial assessment of basic listening and reading skills. Pre- and post-tests monitor progress and measure a learner's ability to apply basic skills in a functional life-skills context. CASAS scores correlate to SPLs and NRS levels.

Earned Income Tax Credit (EITC) Lesson Plans
Karen Dennis, ESL Coordinator
Santa Ana College
School of Continuing Education
Centennial Education Center
2900 West Edinger
Santa Ana, CA 92704
dennis_karen@rsccd.org
714-564-5100

Developed by the School of Continuing Education, Santa Ana College, for use with adult English language learners, these materials are available at no cost.

Jackson, E. (1994). *Non-language outcomes: Activities and resources.* New South Wales, Australia: NSW AMES & National Centre for English Language Teaching and Research.

This guide for teachers of beginning-level English language learners demonstrates how to incorporate learning skills into adult ESL courses. Teaching notes and activities are provided for each objective.

ABOUT THE AUTHOR

A native of England, Brigitte Marshall has gained recognition in the United States for her work integrating workplace know-how skills into language instruction for employment preparation programs. As a consultant with the California Department of Education's Adult Education Office, she has been involved in crafting the state's learner-centered response to the English Literacy and Civics Education initiative. Ms. Marshall is a partner of the Spring Institute for International Studies in Denver, Colorado, for the English Language Training (ELT) Technical Assistance project funded by the federal Office of Refugee Resettlement. The ELT program provided funding for an earlier version of this book.